To

Cheryl Oldfield

Thoughts From the Heart

It is a pleasure
to meet you. We
look forward to seeing
you more often in the
future. Wishing you
continued success always.
With my Best Wishes

Charles S. Haddad

Thoughts

From the Heart

Charles S. Haddad

CHARLCYN PRESS
NEW YORK CITY

Editors: Ellen E. M. Roberts
        Kirsten Neuhaus
Creative Direction and Design: Douglas Wink/Inkway Graphics
Production & Manufacturing: Thomas Nau
Interior Photography: Charles S. Haddad

Published by CharlCyn Press, 100 West 33rd Street, New York, NY 10001.
www.charlcyn.com

FIRST EDITION

Hardcover ISBN 0-9674597-0-2
Paperback ISBN 0-9674597-1-0

Printed in the United States of America

10 9 8 7 6 5 4 3 2 1

*This book is dedicated
to my wife, Cynthia,
the loveliest and most exciting
person in my life.*

*For more than forty years
you have inspired me.*

TABLE OF CONTENTS

INTRODUCTION
by Rachelle Matsas

MY FIRST ENCOUNTER with Charles S. Haddad was in 1993. I received a phone call from Charles explaining he wrote a New Jersey Synagogue newsletter and asked me, Chief Editor of a still young *Image Magazine*, to consider publishing his articles. According to procedure, followed by all new writers, I asked him to fax over copies of his work for my perusal. Thus began a quality business relationship that eventually led to a valued friendship.

Reading Charles' work, I was immediately attracted to his unceasing optimistic outlook and his clear concise writing style. His articles spring from years of life experience that encompass everything from quality relationships, excellent friendships and a strong commitment to business ethics. His works reflect the husband, father, grandfather, friend, businessman, community leader and activist roles that have made up his accomplished life. His love of people and nature; the simple pleasures and his no-nonsense down to earth attitude have made him one of the most popular and beloved writers of *Image Magazine*.

Each month Charles submits his article and asks for my opinion. A perfectionist who is still willing to ask for suggestions is an example of Charles' humility. A man who is always lured by improvement and growth, he is an inspiration to us all. Charles is forever asking if I had any ideas that would enrich his work. The months have eventually turned to years and our professional respect for each other has blossomed like flowers. We have become mutual critics, faxing our work to each other, analyzing and critiquing and always open for opinions and recommendations.

I learned that the enormous respect I have for Charles as a man, an author and a friend is shared by the many people who know him when I was invited by his children to a dedication of a Sefer Torah in honor of Charles and his wife Cynthia. His home and the synagogue were packed to capacity with numerous people who spoke of Charles and all he had accomplished.

As I look back at all *Image* has accomplished I wonder if it could have been possible without the help of Charles. His articles are timeless and his advice unquestionable. *Respect, Prayer, Will Power,* and *Understanding Ourselves* are just some of the titles I've had the pleasure to discover again and again. Charles discusses daily subjects and fills his reader with the optimism that reinforces the fact that each individual is truly special and has the power to achieve and the capability to make a difference.

FOREWORD
by John R. Mangiardi, M.D., F.A.C.S.

WHY IS IT that many wise men, both ancient and modern, become gardeners?

Because they learn to live the metaphor.

Just review the titles that run through this little book, and you will see what I mean. All that it takes to become a true gardener is here: *Simplicity. Achieving Perfection. Learning by Observing. Traditions. Leave Nothing to Chance.* Try growing a garden without all of the above and see how well you do…

An image from my past: My eighty-something grandmother (simple and knowing) gardening. The smell of soil, freshly broken leaves, green everywhere. Kneeling happily with dirt-covered hands and a somehow-clean dress, she would dole out priceless guidance to me while tending to her precious tomatoes.

Things like, "Don't trust a person who doesn't smile even a little on the inside when a baby smiles big on the outside…"

"The world is shrinking, speeding up so fast. You will see. More and more, people will understand less and less…"

These pearls of wisdom did not make a lot of sense at the time to me as a 10-year-old boy, but they are starting to now.

With the next breath she would tell me the correct way to pick a ripe tomato.

Listen to some of Charlie's thoughts:

Every spring, I like to sit on a park bench and kind of catch up with all that is going on.

Confidence is knowing yourself. Many people live a long time and never really get to know themselves.

Speaking up requires the strength to handle stress.

Try thinking in straight lines.

Don't think that just because you are getting older you know enough to stop learning.

My theory that if you are stuck, you have to get yourself out…

If you think life is difficult, try gardening (or even brain surgery): It too can be improved upon only when one keeps it simple, thinks in straight lines, and refuses to stop growing. Of course Charlie is nowhere near eighty. But he is learning how to garden. God bless him in his adventure.

Finding out who you are
and what you want out of life
will help you to get to know yourself.

PART ONE
Getting to Know Yourself

THOUGHTS FROM THE HEART

Tune In To Today

HERE IT IS—ANOTHER DAY. Where to begin? It's very likely that the alarm rings and bingo! Your ears begin to wiggle. Maybe your eyes start to flutter, and you begin to stretch and suddenly realize it's not just a dream.

It's the bell that says get up and go. It's round one in just another day in your life. No, it's not a fifteen-round championship bout. It's the beginning of your day. Can you believe that you've read so much and you're still in bed?

Roll out of bed! The clock is ticking. So much to do. So little time to do it.

As you get yourself ready to rock and roll out of the house, you grab a bite to calm your nerves, before you hit the rush hour traffic one way or another. The sun could be shining. Or it could be raining. If it's snowing, you can think it's bright and clear or you can think it's cold and wet. What's really important is your state of mind.

Many people think about things and events that may take place sometime in the future. The funny thing is that many of these events people worry about never happen. Have you been thinking of future events that affect your feelings? Your focus on future events may make you feel bad, or it may make you feel good. Just remember that most of the things people think are going to happen, one way or another, never take place. So you can temper your daily feelings by taking one day at a time. There's more than enough going on each day for the average person to handle.

First of all, let's get your attitude into perspective. Have your wits about you and begin by appreciating the beauty of the people and places you pass each day. Don't take life for granted because nothing really stays the same forever. What you are enjoying today may not be there tomorrow.

In simple terms, wiggle those ears and tune into today. Give a smile and catch a smile. Have a positive attitude and the day will pass with much satisfaction. Remember, when you learned to walk, you began with a single step!

Why Change?

WHY WOULD ANYONE WANT TO CHANGE? There are so many reasons why you should think about changes in your life. First of all, no one is perfect. Change is necessary to achieve perfection in life. Even though it's hard to change your habits, it's important that you do so for your own happiness. Because happiness is being happy with yourself as well as being happy with those around you.

Did you ever see someone who was so grumpy that he made everyone around him feel the same way? Well, by the time he figured out that he was the cause of their bad feelings, it was too late to change. Just think, if he had had the courage to change, how much happier he could have been. People have a hard time admitting to themselves that they have a deficiency.

But you go through life only once. And once and for all you should change for the better to improve your standard of life and quality of life.

People come from all different backgrounds. You learn to change because of the things you see around you. Why be stubborn to win a point and lose out on a better way of life, which you can create through a change of habits?

Give of yourself and you shall receive back. Remember that you must give with your heart and feel for the next person. Change will come by applying common sense to a given situation. It is up to you and only you to live your life to the best of your capacity. How do you know what to do to change for the better? Trial and error is one way. Analysis of the things you see happening around you is also a good way. The change you make should make good sense to you.

Marriage is the best example when it comes to embracing change. Two people coming from two different families decide they are meant for each other. They get married.

Well, before too long, the honeymoon is over and they must learn to live with each other for the rest of their lives. In order for marriage to work, each partner must accommodate the other. A successful marriage comes about when there is flexibility. The real fun comes when you decide to have a family.

Once you start raising children, you become a psychologist. This is the point where tolerance really plays an important role. You must look beyond to see a reason for change. Times change. Your position in life changes. The toughest thing is to change your thoughts and way of life. Once you have, however, you will be a new person. You will know that you are in control of yourself and will be happier for it.

When children are young, they must be guided sternly and taught the meaning of respect. But when they reach about the age of seventeen, it's time for change. You have to ease up on them or lose them altogether. If your timing is right, you will see it for yourself.

Remember you were once their age and you wanted freedom to think and do as you felt you had to. The truth of the matter is that a better relationship is created by letting go.

Now is a good time to re-evaluate your thoughts about the subject. By taking a position that you feel comfortable with, you can improve your habits and be a happier person.

Organize

I T ALL DEPENDS on how efficient you want to be. Organization of a daily routine is a major benefit for your usage of time. Most people need to be more efficient in utilizing their time. You can start by asking yourself, what are the important things that I have to accomplish today?

You may want to refer to a calendar on which you have all your events listed. Then try to see where there might be time to catch up on other projects. You can write notes on post-its and move them along your calendar from day to day or week to week. Being organized is spending time now to save you from spending more time later. It is anticipation.

Interruptions during the day may cause your original plans to be sidetracked. Examples of interruptions that come to my mind are the telephone ringing, someone walking in, or a meeting that is called without any notice. No matter how many surprises your day brings, it is an advantage to have an agenda to accomplish the more necessary jobs.

Organization of your life will make you more responsible, more productive, and help you grow faster, to earn more sooner. Sounds good doesn't it? Most people in leadership positions are very organized, do not waste words and are busy making decisions on a regular basis. Setting goals and trying to achieve perfection have advantages too. If you think about how efficiently your time is being spent during your current day, you'll probably realize that you could have accomplished more had you laid out the groundwork for the day ahead of time. To help you attain "perfection", try organizing your day's agenda the previous day.

Even a mother's duties have a natural pattern of organization. Her day begins by getting the children up bright and early. Breakfast must be prepared and finally the children are hustled off to school. You know it doesn't end there. Preparing dinner and getting other chores done before the kids are back home from school are just small parts of it. There may be younger babies at home. Time for caring for them is one more thing you need to add to your daily routine. When the children return home from school, it's cookies, milk and homework, followed by bath and dinner. Mom doesn't get a chance to relax until the children go to bed.

While you know that organization of life applies to people who are active, it applies as well to people whose lives have slowed down to retirement. Formulating a regular routine gives a time to each task, and a task for each time. Getting up early and getting out to exercise, play golf, or even take up something in the way of continuing education are some options. Whether you are a busy young mom, or a retired grandparent, when you have a routine, life has much more meaning.

Using your time efficiently gives you a sense of accomplishment. By taking advantage of time will result in life being a happy event for you each day. You may go to bed tired, but for sure it will feel good just thinking about how much you've done.

Achieving Perfection

HOW WOULD YOU DEFINE perfection in your life? This can be a very complicated question. Everybody knows this is not a perfect world. Once you realize this, you have much to think about.

Trying to achieve a goal relates to perfection in the fact that you have the ability to get the job done. On the other hand, you may not always do something perfectly. This is not something to feel bad about. "Nothing ventured, nothing gained," as the saying goes.

In life we come in contact daily with many different people and personalities. Begin with your own personality. What does it take for you to get along with others? Are you shy or are you outgoing? Do you really try or are you secretly lazy? Most people are somewhere in the middle.

Trying to be friendly toward the next person is always a good beginning. Showing an interest in the feelings of others is another great way to get started. Respect towards the other person will show a good feeling for both parties.

You should not expect to act perfectly. No one is perfect. We all make mistakes. You won't always get the same reception from the other person that you offer to that person, though in most cases, you will. Remember, if this doesn't happen, it's okay because no situation is perfect either. Admitting to yourself or someone else that you have made a mistake is a very important point. It takes a big person to admit a mistake and an even bigger person to make an apology.

Everyone must strive to make things happen through his personality. People make their own personalities by their very actions. A person creates his or her own personality. So get to work if you want to enjoy life to the fullest.

A person has to live with herself. The more people hide their feelings within themselves, the more they become unhappy with themselves. It's like a breath of fresh air: if you take a deep breath and then let it out, how does that feel? You've released a bit of anxiety in yourself. You feel good about the smell of the fresh air you are breathing now. This is pretty much the way it is in life. Getting things off your chest is often a big relief. When you have shared a problem with someone, it is almost as though you have solved it.

Don't feel that you have to go through life alone. Perfection does not mean that much. In fact, nobody's perfect. Being able to understand your shortcomings are part of growing up and being a part of the grown-up world.

Life can be like sports, where you try to meet the challenge. Not too many athletes become the best. Most people who play sports are happy just to be in the game.

People move along continuously in time. Even when things are perfect, they change the next moment. It isn't worth it to let things that aren't perfect bother you, because they have little meaning in the overall picture of your life. Let your heart lead the way to your goals. Learning how to minimize your shortcomings will amount to perfection in your life.

P.S.—The water in my shower was the perfect temperature this morning!

Confidence

ONE THING LEADS TO THE NEXT, or at least, that's how it seems. You go with the flow when you have confidence in your abilities. Getting a job done and doing it over and over gets you into shape. You fine-tune it in a natural pattern once you have done it often enough.

Confidence is knowing yourself. Many people never really get to know themselves. To find out what you are all about, look at what others think of you. You are reflected by others who see you as you really are.

It's hard to explain, but I went through this reflective experience several years ago. I had been taking a course at Dale Carnegie in public speaking and human relations. At the end, the instructor passed around comment cards. Each one had the name of a student in the class to be evaluated from the time we spent together. Each of us put one or two lines about each of the other forty students. I was amazed at the comments on my card. People who never said anything to my face were saying very nice things about me! This is because people by nature do not want to reveal the good things they see in others. But try doing this and you will also learn about yourself.

Seeing good in others and mentioning it is an art. It must be done carefully. Otherwise the person you are praising may think he is being buttered up. Say it naturally, spontaneously—and the next time someone pays you a compliment, you can say you learned something about yourself.

There is no greater experience than telling people about the good qualities you see in them. Even if they know it, they feel good that you know it too. Give and you shall receive in kind. Love is understood, but when the word is spoken and the feeling is there, just imagine the difference. Try it!

I'd have to say I had never really never known myself until I was forty. Don't be surprised. Most people really do not know their own identities. People are all built the same way. Next time you go to a party you may not feel confident. You may be asking yourself: Do I know these people? How will they act? Will I feel comfortable? You are as vulnerable as the next person. Look at the other people and say to yourself "Why should I feel inadequate? People really are all the same." Getting to know the other people is the real challenge. The more confidence you have, the easier it is to reach out to others. Nothing else should really matter.

Confidence is the feeling you get from the picture you put in your mind about a given situation. So from now on, use the fastest film and the finest camera to take the best picture possible.

Self-Esteem

EVERYONE NEEDS IT. The dictionary definition reads "Belief in yourself. Self-respect. Pride in oneself." To me the best definition of "self-esteem" is "a sense of one's own dignity or worth." In daily life, we take pride in our achievements. Pride is a feeling that soothes us. You can call it satisfaction.

When you can believe in yourself, you can feel like a new person. The confidence that goes with self-esteem makes it easier for others to like you as well. Positive thinking has a lot to do with believing in yourself. Somehow, if you believe in something strongly enough, you can make it happen.

Believing in yourself may start out as a dream. It may not even be real. To me, it is like planting a seed and watching it grow. It doesn't grow fast. Just think of your life as you grow from stage to stage: it is a slow process. Those who are fortunate enough to have more patience than others will reap the harvest. Self-respect in itself is something that you can build on over a period of many years. It is a course that you must choose early in life.

The dictionary definition implies that you must have respect for yourself and for your own character and reputation. Your character develops from the things that you see around you and your reactions to them.

Your reputation is also part of a pattern of self-reflection. You can have a reputation for honesty, or helpfulness. Underlying these fine traits is a sound footing, a positive outlook on life. Sure, it's easy to say, but it's up to you to make it happen. Life is really a dream that comes to fruition. The result of the seeds that you sow throughout life.

Love life and you will love yourself and others around you.

Need I say more? Short and sweet—life is really simple in its way. Just look up the definition of self-esteem or create your own definition for yourself. See how it works in practice. A little effort on your part will go a long way.

P.S.—Smile for a while and you'll be in style.

Improving Your Attitude

MANY PEOPLE ARE PLAGUED with an attitude problem. The main reason for this is they don't even realize that they have a problem.

Life passes by too quickly and you should determine if your attitude is offensive to others. If you have an attitude that is defensive, try understanding why you feel uncomfortable, or maybe even grouchy or edgy at times.

To be more explicit, attitude has to do with the manner in which one speaks. No one likes to be spoken to in a condescending or bossy manner.

Attitude is expressed by the way a person says things. It is in the voice tone. Usually, people speaking with an attitude are on the defensive.

To improve your attitude towards others, try speaking in a soft, positive tone. You will see the difference in how people react to you. To your amazement, they will be receptive. Your life will change and you will be much happier.

Most people will not tolerate another person's overbearing attitude. Life is not easy. No one ever said it would be. Understanding yourself is even more complex. It is up to each individual who has a negative attitude to recognize it.

Wanting to be a winner and to be liked by others depends on your attitude. If you have a negative attitude and are fortunate enough to realize it, try thinking positively as a beginning towards a happier life, for you and the people around you.

Try starting your day with a smile. Let it last for at least a mile. Keep smiling for a happier you.

Getting Through Life

TRAINING YOURSELF for the real world takes lots of energy. The commitment to going forward and being productive is essential to success in business.

First, you should have your sights set to be honest and ethical. This means you must create habits that will be acceptable as you go through life.

Honesty means being true to yourself as well as to others. While you are still in school, your ethics will show in your approach towards tasks, like studying, that come your way daily. There are no shortcuts. Studying for a test means putting the time in to make a good grade. Anyone can copy from someone else, but how much will you learn?

Going to college is a stepping stone which gives you needed time to adjust to an adult world. It is an opportunity to make friends. In college, you can meet all kinds of people. This gives you practice judging them while they are judging you.

Your honesty will grow with you as you go through life. It is an essential ingredient for success. As the saying goes "Everyone knows everyone—no one fools anyone." Therefore, it makes sense to treat others as you would like to be treated. Taking shortcuts is choosing the easy way over the right way. But if you do things the right way the first time, just think of the time you save by not having to do them over. Measuring your success in terms of good ethics, you will have something to build on. In business as an adult, you will grow faster than you ever could have imagined.

Part of good ethics is being honest with yourself. You owe it to yourself to find something that you want to do for the rest of your life and stay with it. The person who changes paths too often will feel like she is starting out all over again, and she will be. Time is everything. Each person only has so much of it.

You are young only once. Your energies are greatest in your youth. Take full advantage of them and continue to be young at heart as you go through life. It will extend your youth as well as your interest in life.

Develop Your Own Personality And Character That Works For You!

Silence is Golden— To a Point!

PEOPLE GO THROUGH LIFE on a day-to-day basis. They let many things go by that they disagree with. However, when it comes to speaking up, people are afraid, maybe because they don't want to rock the boat.

There are two kinds of people. The first is the uninhibited type, a free thinker and a person who speaks his mind. The second type is an individual whose philosophy is "silence is golden." This personality is self-conscious, lacks confidence, and avoids aggression. The first type is more adept at handling stress than the second. There are many reasons for this phenomenon. Feelings of self-confidence and inner strength are essential tools. Knowledge and experience are also advantages in stressful situations, regardless of personality type.

Speaking up requires the strength to handle stress. People who tend to weaken easily are never able to really express what is on their minds.

The inability to fully express feelings is unhealthy, especially for people involved in a relationship. This inability only helps to create stress. By essentially holding your feelings inside of you, an uncomfortable and awkward feeling is the only result. Instead of focusing on the trouble at hand you begin to imagine other things that are going wrong. Silence in turn creates depression. In this case the steadfast philosophy "Silence is golden" does not apply.

The first point to understand is that not even a loved one can read your mind. For someone to know what you are thinking, or what is troubling you, you must be willing to communicate. When the person knows what is on your mind, he can then respond and help. Until that happens, you can only feel helpless. Imagine being stuck on an island and trying to find a way off. Where can you go without a boat and a paddle? Not very far.

People need to experience many different situations before the pressure of stress is alleviated. Releasing anger or frustration that builds up inside you is both productive and beneficial. How far will you get by holding your thoughts and feelings within your bodily confines?

When it comes to self-confidence and peace of mind, you should practice on a dally basis to clear your mind of negative thoughts. All problems that are bothering you should be released. Try instead to focus on the positive.

You can begin by trying to improve your powers of self-control. Speak up to others when you think the time is right. Be calm and diplomatic, with an attitude of openness and ease. It is by far healthier to speak your mind than to hold your feelings inside of you.

Remember: silence is golden…to a point!

What Makes People Successful

WHERE ARE YOU AT IN LIFE? If you are just starting out and have graduated from high school or college, you are probably still formulating your ideas as to what you want to do with the rest of your life. This would be a good time to ask the advice of an older person you respect and have confidence in. Being independent and responsible early on will give you the opportunity to grow faster. Those of you with a mind of your own, who take action with the right luck and timing, will find out sooner than others what it means to become successful in life.

What I have found to be true, is that commitment and strong will are the ingredients for individual success. Try to take these two qualities apart, so you can analyze their particular attributes.

Whatever you choose to do, you must make a commitment to devote the amount of time needed to develop the necessary skills. When things are new, it takes time to adapt to them. Don't expect to rush things along without the proper foundation and understanding. There are no real short cuts when it comes to a profession. You must put in the time like all successful people had to when they started out.

If your heart is in it, you will be able to see things through. This is the basis for having a strong will. It means having a positive attitude towards whatever you are involved in, and being the driving force behind accomplishing your own goals. If you can remain strong, even in the face of disappointment or failure, you will gradually become an inspiration to others around you. People like to be around others who have determination and drive. It often rubs off on them because competition brings out the best in all of us.

People who are successful realize it once they achieve their status in life. I always believed in trying to reach for the sky and always wound up achieving more than I could expect. Setting high standards will give you a better chance to succeed at what you want to achieve.

This is true not just in achieving financial success, but success in any aspect of life. Is it any less true when a boy and a girl are searching for a spouse? You must set high standards for yourself in order to be happy with the results.

It is up to you to achieve your own goals in life. It is your own standard that you must live up to. Never lose sight of your vision but also be able to focus on the big picture and you will have all the ingredients for success.

Competition

COMPETITION gives you the incentive to want to do better. Even people who don't think they are competing, sometimes do so unknowingly. Because in truth, we are always competing with ourselves. The best example I can think of is when I'm playing golf, I am really competing against my own ability to hit that ball a mile and sink that putt and smile.

Competition is important in games, sports, even business. The old saying goes "Competition creates business." If six stores on the block carry Fruit of the Loom® underwear, they'll all do business. The store owners need the famous brand to help draw the customer into their store. In sports, everyone likes to be on the winning team. But, they must perform as a team in order to win as a team.

But the reality is that although you will not always win, you should never quit. Being a good loser is almost as good as winning. Because our lives are not like those of the Olympians. They train throughout their youth, and if they don't win the gold medal one year, they have to wait another four years to try again. We can dream everyday and excel in every way, whenever we have something to compete for. Each mistake you make can teach you something that you can try out the next time.

Once you finish schooling you can almost feel like you are in a fish bowl until you find yourself. One way of formulating your ideas and your future is to look up to someone who successful in the career you are interested in. Try finding the ingredients that made this person achieve success.

But don't forget about what your colleagues can teach you. Working well with others is very important. It gives you the opportunity to learn from one another, while you are helping each other. The advantage of being open-minded and helpful towards others is that you can gain new experiences and knowledge. Because the best way to learn, is to go through it. And everything is a little easier if you have someone to help you and encourage you. So do positive things for yourself and others, and you will eventually benefit from them.

So short and sweet—competition keeps us going. Welcome the opportunity to compete and make the most of it. Always try your best, even if it looks like you might not win. Don't be afraid of competition because it gives you a motivation to improve your opportunities and goals. Giving it all you have, versus short-changing yourself, will make all the difference in succeeding.

Remember, it's really up to you. Don't expect someone else to make you look good. It just doesn't happen that way.

P.S.—Win, lose, or draw, keep right on smiling.

Exercise

TRY NOT TO GET TIRED FROM DOING NOTHING. Does that sound familiar? To begin with, people are only human. They have to care for their bodies. When the days are longer, the early daylight causes me to get up early in the morning. What better way to start my day than by exercising? Exercise might be the ticket for you as well.

First of all, it gets the creaks out of your body. Try doing some stretching. Exercising properly is very important. You should get professional instructions on how to stretch. You can do more harm than good if you don't warm up before you exert yourself. Walking is the most common form of exercise today. Walking loosens up your body while building muscles, especially for the heart. The oxygen is pumped through your system causing your nostrils to open up. So, in any type of exercise you do, you should warm up by walking slowly for about five minutes. This lets the blood circulate around the muscles and helps to loosen them.

You should walk from twenty minutes to a half-an-hour to work off some body fat. Walk at a pace that is comfortable for you. A cool-down period of about five minutes at the end of your walk is also necessary. This helps to calm the body's muscles.

Walking has many hidden benefits. It helps to increase the good cholesterol. It's great for the heart. It is also very exhilarating. Try taking a cold shower afterwards and see how refreshing it feels.

I cannot overstate the advantage of exercise. It's true that it is hard work. At the same time, there are not many things that you can appreciate that come easy. So get with it and schedule some kind of exercise at least three times a week.

Toning your body will keep you feeling younger longer. Think of the word mold. It sounds like something old. You don't want to turn into mold, do you? Think young, feel young, and you will be, by exercising regularly.

Will Power

THE STRENGTH TO CONTROL YOURSELF and the self-discipline that gives you firmness of mind is called will power. Believe it or not, all human beings possess will power.

Having will power is the first step. Knowing how to use it to your advantage is the second step. You need to give will power serious consideration because only by believing in yourself can you follow your will through to completion.

Will power is in reality a mind game. I know that many times when it comes to food I can easily indulge in something that looks very tempting. I know that if I have a certain kind of dessert either my health or my waistline is at risk. For me, finding my will power when I sit down to eat a delicious sweet is a standard routine. To be successful with will power, you will need to think about an issue on a regular basis, just as I do with sweets. By keeping your will power on your mind, you will have good results.

Independence plays an important part in will power. In a sense, using your independence to choose a job and then the will power to make it succeed go hand-in-hand. You and only you make the final decision about what you do. You have the ability to do whatever you want. However, you have to choose to use it.

Recognizing your weaknesses is another important part of will power. When something bothers you, you can write down on a small piece of paper what you would like to do in order to overcome the weakness. By doing this you have created a reminder for yourself to correct this shortcoming and eventually you will feel better about yourself.

Personally, I keep the paper in my back pocket and look at it at least twice a day. It is easy to forget things during a busy day. When I write things down, and make it a habit to look at it twice a day, remembering becomes easier. It becomes a system that I can count on to get results. You can use this same system, so that your will power is in place for you to make it work for you.

Naturally, will power can be be applied in many different cases. Apply will power to your needs. Make sure you understand what it can mean to you. You will also find out how much you have gained personally by using your will power to benefit yourself and others around you. Trying to get a job done? Use will power!

Will power can be used to control anger. Will power is being able to control yourself by learning to listen to others before speaking. These are just some examples of your convictions creating self-control.

In the end, will power is simply knowing what is best for you. Spread the word to friends and family what will power has done for you after you have applied some of these principles. Give will power a try and find out what will power can do for you.

*Getting along with others
is the first step in getting along with yourself.*

PART TWO
Getting Along With Others

People And Politics

WE ALL HAVE TO PLAY THE GAME. No, I'm not talking about election politics. But the real business of daily life, which consists of the daily political interplay between people. You and me, mother and daughter, father and son, brother and sister, worker and co-worker. I guess we could go on and on.

With your family for instance, children and parents must find a way to communicate and compromise. Sometimes children will talk to their mom in hopes that she will act as a go between to dad and vice versa. Sometimes brother will offer to do his sister's chore in return for a chance to pick the television show they watch. These are all examples of politics at home. Each member of the family needs the other in order for the family to work. Each member has a special influence on the other. And each member of a family has something they want or need from the other. With big or small bargains, remember that you win some and you lose some. But the more persistent you are, the more successful you will be.

In business, being able to get along with others, or play the game, is also essential. Give and take should be the order of the day. But you must always remember that seniority has a meaningful advantage. The boss is still the boss. He or she deserves your respect as the head of your office. Just as mom and dad have the final say at home, so the boss has the final say at work. And people always appreciate others who show them respect and courtesy.

Someday, you might be forced into taking a stand on a given situation or asked to take sides. This is a very tricky business, because you don't want to lose the respect of the people on the side you don't choose. So think carefully and take the time to size up the entire situation. Make sure that your choice will be beneficial to the entire cause (at home or at the office). In order to rectify a difference of opinion that cannot be easily resolved, you may have to reevaluate the situation. It might be beneficial to agree for the present time only to wait and see if the situation improves. You never want to win the battle and lose the war.

So you see, politics do have a place in everyday life. Understanding ways of getting along with others is always to your advantage. And learning to be diplomatic with others is not unlike real politics. You must have patience, time, and motivation in order to succeed in life. The key is to play fair, always treat people with respect, and compromise to get what you want.

The key to the political game is learning how to play it. Good luck in your endeavors. Just remember to be diplomatic in your ways and it will always pay off.

Transition

THINK BACK TO WHEN YOU WERE YOUNG and growing up. How were you treated or mistreated? Some adults can not forget how they were treated during their childhoods. They go through life remembering the things that bothered them. But do we truly realize when we mistreat our children? Who is closer to you than your own child? Do you think about the child's feelings toward you when you punish them harshly or unjustly? Verbally abusing or striking a child is not an answer. These actions are demeaning and will have a lasting effect upon the child's mind. They will cause the child to feel out of control and suffer from low self-confidence. They will always be questioning themselves, "What did I do wrong to deserve that?"

Children's young minds develop quickly. They are taught much more today at a younger age and can absorb a lot more than we did at the same age. Things happen faster today. The daily pressures are greater. The demands to succeed are greater. They learn the good and not so good, sometimes not knowing which is correct. This makes our job that much more important. Parents have a tremendous impact on their children. They want and need someone to look up to. It is important for people raising children to realize that they affect the minds and the future of their children in a direct way. Don't let time take its toll. Let time be marked by understanding and progress.

Teaching a child independence and responsibility are the most important things a parent can give a child. These are tools the child will need to go out into the real world to perform his or her talents and to be successful. Forcing a child to do something that they may feel they don't want to do is the wrong approach. Put the idea in his or her mind first and see how it is accepted. Teach a child to make decisions. Look around you and you will notice many adults that do not know how to make decisions. This is because the parents made all the decisions for them and when it was the child's turn the child didn't know how to make one.

The next important stage in time is graduation from grade school to high school. This is a major step in the growth of a child. The child goes through many changes, both mentally and physically. This stage must be well understood by the parent. The child is about to be influenced by many outside forces. You should change your views and your attitude at this point while guiding your child very sensitively. Children start to realize who they are and question it at the same time. In the formative years at the age of 16 or 17, a teenager needs space. In some cases if you don't give it to them, you will lose them. You must be the judge.

The next stage is college or work. Study prepares you for the real world. At this point all the responsibility and independence you have given your child over the years while marking time will pay off for everyone.

You can look forward to being a proud parent as you watch your child grow to become a successful adult. You can take pride that you did the right things by being as sensitive toward your child's feelings as you would like he or she to be toward yours.

You can look at raising a child as a two way street. Give and take becomes a way of life.

Who Are You and Who Am I?

D ISCOVERING WHO I AM, as an individual and as a member of society, is one of the most difficult and interesting challenges I have ever faced. How often do you get to reflect on your feelings? Very little of my identity was explained to me in the developing years of grade school. I had to pick up ideas about myself on my own. But I discovered an even bigger part of my identity through feedback given to me by people I have interacted with. As an example, several years ago I took a course in public speaking. I felt that since I spoke publicly often, I might do a better job of speaking if I took a course. I guess I was looking to have more confidence in my ability to speak publicly. It was a great course for me. I made many friends. It's the type of course where you really get to know each other. Your true personality comes out.

In the time frame of fourteen classes lasting three and a half hours each, you had the chance to get to know each other enough to give an analysis of each other. Every student takes center stage every week. The last session of the course was graduation. After we all had taken three minutes to speak on any subject, the professor gave each of us blank index cards. We each wrote our names at the top of the card. He then asked us to hand the card to the students around us, and asked each of us to write in one or two sentences about what we saw in that person.

It was very interesting to see what other people saw in me. It sure gave me a better understanding of myself. It felt good to know that I could make an impact on so many people In such a short time. I wish more people had the opportunity I had. I suggest schools should have some sort of review during the term for the students, at which time their contemporaries review the positive points of each person in the class on index cards. You can even use the idea as a family game. Just think of it as lots of fun. Who knows you better than your own family?

The way I look at it, other people help to give you the confidence that you need in life. You have to treat others in a positive manner. Anyone can be negative. A compliment is something many people do not know how to give or accept. When you are able to accept a compliment you will be able to accept that feeling of gratification that comes with it. When someone tells you that you did a good job, it enforces the good feelings of accomplishment as well as confidence In yourself. You can enjoy saying thank you.

Everything must be based on positive feedback. Look at everyone's bright side and bring it out. Practice it on your friends and they may return some good thoughts to you.

Because life can be very rewarding for the individual that wants to know more about himself or herself. It's never too late in life to learn about yourself. Take a course on any subject that you feel you are lacking in. Discover your true personality and find out how you perceive yourself to be in the real world.

The real world can be surprising and fun, or disruptive and cruel. But if you know who you are, you can face each new challenge with confidence. And each reward you earn will be a positive affirmation of you. By taking the time to analyze who you are, you can learn to connect to your deepest feelings, and your deepest thoughts to a positive, happy, holistic you!

Experience

HAVE YOU EVER SAT DOWN and thought that you had a handle on things? Every once in a while I will think I have got it figured out, the road ahead of me is smooth and clear. But just as I sit back to relax and enjoy the calm, surprise! A new event or person will come into my life and everything will change again. Life doesn't stand still, so you have to be ready for changes. The best edge you can have for changing times is experience. Experience will give you clues on how to react to things, and what will happen next. The more experience you have, the better prepared you are for what comes next. Unfortunately, something so valuable can never be acquired second-hand. Try telling someone to protect themselves from something that has happened to you. You will never forget the feeling and they probably won't remember what you told them.

But this is not to say that you can't learn a lot from those who have seen more and done more. You just have to learn to listen a little harder. I look up to my elders that have really experienced life. They are like fine wine, becoming more valuable as they get older. With an open mind, our younger generation will have the advantage of taking the good out of life's experiences from their elders.

The next generation will be more inclined to listen to you if you stay young at heart. It is important not to forget what it feels like to be young. Keeping and being young is a matter of the mind. The impressions adults convey should always be related to the younger generation, and how their decisions will affect their own future and their children's. It is up to us to impress the feeling of our experience to each generation.

The strength of our young ones must come from the parents and the elders while the youngsters are growing into adulthood. Our experience of life will play a key role. Being there for them when they need you can make the difference in your life and theirs.

P.S.—We all must pay a price for experience. Most people learn by paying for it in one way or another.

Having a Sense of Humor

A SENSE OF HUMOR is something you can strive for. Some people are just too serious all the time. People with an ongoing sense of humor can still be taken seriously. One way of getting a point across is to bring it out with humor. You don't necessarily have to be serious to get your point across to someone else. Sometimes a smile and a good joke can have the positive impact that will lighten up the feelings of people around you.

Have you ever noticed a good politician when he speaks? Most of the time they seem relaxed and will mix humor with their politics in order to lighten up the audience while getting their attention. Once you have the attention of an audience, then you can get your ideas into their minds.

Just think how dull life would be without a sense of humor. As a rule I practice it regularly, in the home, at the office, and with my grandchildren and friends. Because humor makes for good clean fun as well as a good relationship with everyone. It also keeps me young at heart, just trying to keep up with the younger people around me.

Because most people are too concerned about what others think, they tend to be inhibited, and therefore hold back their true feelings. The key is to be loose and feel free to express your true feelings. Just be yourself. Be natural and do what comes naturally in a given situation. This is the key to humor. You must be comfortable with yourself in order to be comfortable with others. If you are open and honest about who you are, the next person will be honest and free with you too.

To all of you that are interested in learning to have a sense of humor, look around at the people you come in contact with daily. You can easily study and learn the various techniques people use for humor; notice how they gain your attention.

Life is a continuous learning experience. Enjoy your life to the fullest. And try using some humor to brighten up each day.

Now lets get serious and learn to live with a sense of humor.

Communicating With Others

THE KEY TO SUCCESS is learning how to communicate with others. It is by learning when to speak and when to listen that you can truly work with others towards a common goal. The most important step in this lesson is not interrupting other people when they are talking. If you do that, a person's train of thought is lost, the conversation changes and maybe you just lost the opportunity to learn something that would have been beneficial to you. Besides, others are so grateful when you listen to what they say, it makes them feel needed, and they will be more inclined to listen to you. So next time a thought pops in your head and you feel like blurting it out, try to put what you want to say next on hold, until the opportunity arises.

Another form of communication is the pen. A very powerful way of getting your point across. Many times a letter may be a more effective communicator than a phone call. You can take the time to be clearer by giving more thought to what you want to say. The recipient also has the opportunity to sit quietly to digest what is written in the letter. A phone call does not give a person the same opportunity. On the phone, there could be interruptions or distractions which would prevent someone from giving you their full attention. Writing someone a letter also gives you a good reason to call him or her. It gives you a better opportunity to discuss the subject about which you wrote. The person you are writing to will have had time to give it some thought, and may have some ideas of their own as well.

Whichever way you choose, communication is a necessary ingredient for getting along with people. The best way to ensure communication will continue, is to keep an open mind and never be too quick to judge or dismiss others. Everyone has something to say, so if you pay attention, what you learn might be well worth the effort.

Respect Begins at Home

BABE RUTH, KING OF BASEBALL, for many years, broke all kinds of home run records. He was a hero of his time and he commanded respect. But he was also a special human being, because with all the respect he commanded, he still had humility. He kept his feet on the ground and never lost touch of who he was. He valued his fellow man. Because of this, he earned their respect. He is a perfect example of a man who gave respect, and received it.

But being respectful of others must be learned. Just as you must learn to appreciate music or art, you have to learn to appreciate people. And the best way to begin this lesson is as a child. You have two choices. To train them or to spoil them. If you love them and wish your child a good life, you must give them the proper training. It is up to you to teach them to say please and thank you. They look to you for guidance. You have to teach them to respect their parents and themselves. The second one is just as important. It will instill self-confidence in the child. Also, if a parent expects to be respected by their children, they must also show that they respect their children.

Parents showing respect for each other is the best example for a child to learn from. At the age of thirteen, each of my children wrote down for me on paper what they felt respect meant to them. It had the natural impact of making them more aware of it. I might add that what they wrote made me very proud of them. What children see at home is what they take with them when they leave home and are far away from your protection. We are all examples for others around us.

For marriage to be successful, the partners must have a mutual respect for one another. A man and woman marry because of love. But as the saying goes, "you can't live on love". Respect for one another is essential for a marriage to succeed and for a couple to have a happy life together. It is the happy result of giving each other space and understanding individual wishes.

In the workplace, you must also earn the respect of others. When you're starting out, remember how many years your new associates have been working. Their experience, based on their performance has already been recognized. It is now your turn to prove yourself. Being able to get along with others and showing the proper respect for others will indicate how successful you will be in the working world. Keep in mind that you can learn a lot from people around you when starting out.

But you cannot buy respect. It must be earned. I've met a lot of great people in our community over the years. The nicest thing that I can say about them is that they gave me the chance to gain their respect over the years. Because it taught me that respect can not be pressed upon someone, but takes time and patience. But when you finally feel that someone respects you, you know that respect is firm and well-founded.

As we grow up, we learn to get up and say hello to our elders. A friendly hello and a nice smile will go a long way. A firm handshake is also a very important sign of respect. It doesn't take that long for us to become the elders. Everyone pays his dues in life.

The key to succeeding in life is to respect everyone. Everyone is important, special and unique in her own way. We have as individuals the opportunity to reach greatness and feel good about it. Having respect for others with humility and being honest and true to yourself can only bring you happiness. We as people can feel good knowing that we have earned the respect of others.

Salesmanship

NO MATTER what your career or position in life, you will find that you are always trying to sell something to someone. Most of your life you will be selling yourself and your ideas to others. You may not have thoughts about it but salesmanship is a factor, even in early childhood, more or less from about 1 year of age. If a baby cries in some cases, it means he or she wants attention. Once the baby has your attention, then the baby will try to get their idea of what they want across. As parents, grandparents, and relatives we are easily convinced. It's when they get older that selling becomes more complicated.

Getting into the finer points of salesmanship: Once you really get involved in the business world and are making a living from it, this is when your ability to sell really counts.

You learn a lot about selling from others around you. The first point is to be honest. People want to believe you but won't be easily fooled. If you like the product you are selling, it will show, and you will convince others easily. When trying to sell, always think about the buyer and how that person will feel about your presentation.

I grew up learning three methods of selling, the hard sell, the soft sell, and the fast sell. You can imagine the confusion of seeing and learning all three types of selling? Well I was more fortunate than I realized. Because now I am able to combine all three at the same time. First be prepared. Keep in mind what your customer may have a need for. Study the details of your presentation. To be successful, you must be knowledgeable. Second, always make it easy for the customer. If there is extra work to do, make sure you do it yourself. Thirdly, hard sell should be the last effort you make. You must be very careful when using hard sell. You do not want to reach the point where you alienate the buyer. This is a very sensitive kind of selling. You must be sincere in your efforts.

Fast sell is a combination of both. The buyer usually has only so much time. Therefore, you must fast sell. This comes into play when you have prepared for your meeting with enough knowledge to move through your presentation quickly and efficiently.

You should also try to recognize a customer's unique personality and then customize your sales pitch to it. Adaptability is the key thing to keep in mind. Sincerity and thinking continuously of what you can do to make a customer happy will show that you care about the interaction and the result.

The best way to learn sales is from a true professional. A true professional is a person with experience that has learned to combine the necessary ingredients needed to make a smooth, sincere, and effective presentation.

Most buyers will look forward to working with someone who transmits an honest interest in their needs. Just realize that practice makes perfect presentations and will bring positive results.

Negotiation

NEGOTIATION IS A SKILL that is acquired over time. It is the art of give-and-take discussions. It can be used in business. It can be used in family matters. It can be used in many instances that may come up in your life. Using negotiation does not necessarily mean you will come out ahead. Disagreements between two people cannot always be worked out to the satisfaction of both parties.

The key element is flexibility. Willingness on the part of both parties to give and take a little creates a balance for a successful conclusion. Diplomacy is a related part of negotiation. Diplomats actually negotiate daily as a way of life. Negotiation is the art where they have achieved their expertise. Being diplomatic in conversation is being able to look at both sides for a better understanding of a situation and coming up with a solution that will work for all parties involved.

In sales, I find that I am constantly trying to improve my negotiating techniques. I actually see the beneficial results of negotiation every day. Understanding the thinking and the ways of an individual always gives me a better perception of how to win at negotiating every time. I have to give a little to get a lot. I'll share some of my techniques with you so that you will be known as a hot shot.

Negotiation can be as simple a situation as getting your children to do the things they should be doing. Or it can be as complex as an international incident involving hostages. Take, for example, the hostage negotiation. The very safety of the hostage is at stake. Care in the words that are spoken must be very delicately thought out. I use this example because it is the extreme. It is to reinforce the need for all of us to understand how critical it is in whatever we negotiate to keep a cool head.

You can do this by give-and-take and by letting the other person think he has won. It is important that you gain the trust of all parties involved. Honesty and sincerity in negotiating will produce very effective results. If you go through life analyzing your attributes, you will better understand your ability to negotiate a better life for yourself.

Let's face it! You can't win without trying. Your tools are a cool head, care in the words you use and a knowledge of diplomacy. Good luck!

Respect for One Another

IF THERE IS ANY NEW YEAR'S RESOLUTION that I can recommend, it would be that we try to have a better understanding of the next person. A simple smile or a friendly hello to the next person has no cost. The real return is on your investment. When a person does wrong and they find it hard to apologize, does that person realize how small of a concession they are making when they apologize? The best thing a person can do is the smallest thing. It is such a small thing to ask if you really care. Remember, try not to make the small things big by not thinking of the next person's feelings in the New Year.

May you all be blessed with peace of mind, happiness, and prosperity in the New Year...because you care!

This was a speech given on the Eve of Yom Kippur.

Raising Children

Parenthood is a very delicate matter. The expression goes "You only get out of them what you put into them." Our children's reactions are a direct result of the image and actions that they see in their parents. The influence of a parent has no limits. If you raise a good child, it's because you, the parents, worked hard to give them good character. Honesty, integrity and love are just some of the ingredients a parent must give a child.

Raising a child properly means spending as much time with your child as possible. You have an investment in their future. Nothing about the basics ever changes. Courtesy and manners are essential to instill in a child. Kids today have many positive and negative influences in their lives. What they learn from you will be mixed with what they learn from their friends and the media. Giving your children a warm and happy home life will give them a stronger foundation with which to fend off peer pressure. Nothing in life is easy, but you can teach your children that doing things the right way, pays off in the end.

Even if you can afford to give them everything they want, you really can't afford to give them whatever they want. Buying them the big cars and expensive vacations is no way to teach them the values that they will need to carry on their lives. Appreciation for the good things in life should be earned. It's the job of the parents to inspire their children and explain to them that it's a competitive world out there. Don't let them find out after it's too late.

It seems that we have almost come full circle. Times change because of the times.

P.S.—Just realize how precious your children are and you will appreciate how unimportant material things can be. Love and caring attention will go a long way.

A Dozen Ways to Spoil Your Child

1. Don't force her to do anything she doesn't want to do. You don't want to frustrate her, do you?

2. Always defend him against teachers, police, neighbors and other kids. They don't understand him—in fact, they can't even STAND him.

3. Let her choose what she wants to eat. She knows what's best for her from watching Saturday morning cartoon shows.

4. Don't let him earn things the way you had to. Give him everything he wants—before he even asks.

5. Make sure he knows how MORE or LESS his parents earn than the other parents he knows. This will help him figure out whether he is underprivileged.

6. Never, under any circumstances, make her help around the house. After all, she wasn't brought in to this world to work for you.

7. Never tell him how hard you work. He might be sorry for you, and you don't want to make him unhappy even for a moment.

8. Give up all your interests and friends in favor of hers. All kids need a forty-year-old pal.

9. Shower her with presents to show you love her. Material things—lots of presents—are the best way of showing you love her.

10. Keep him out of school any time he hasn't finished his homework. Be sure to show him how to forge your name—forgery is a great career choice!

11. Who needs a parent? Make sure that you ingratiate yourself to your child to justify your existence in her life.

12. Don't make your child anxious by making him wait. Always serve him his dinner first, and never let anyone else talk when he has something he wants to say.

Inspiration

LIFE CAN BE EXASPERATING AT TIMES. People have their ups and downs. After all, you're only human. It takes a good look at the surrounding environment to help understand what makes people happy. In a two-part melody each singer inspires the other. I get the same feeling singing in synagogue. In life, just as in music, the power of inspiration is hidden—waiting there to be discovered.

Inspiration is what gets me going. Just knowing that there's someone out there waiting to be helped is motivation enough for me. Writing to you, whether you realize it or not, has been very inspiring to me—I can share my feelings with you in such a plain and simple way.

When you can get the feeling across to someone and convince him in some way to change his ways for the better, you can say you have been inspirational to that person. To me there is no greater power—the key to inspiration is to be mentally fixed on the idea of wanting to help others. Everyone goes through life in a similar fashion. Everyone has an allowance of 24 hours a day to spend. What kind of value one derives out of these 24 hours depends on the individual.

Just think of all the good things you can do for others by inspiring them to appreciate themselves for one reason or another. Thinking of others should be a full-time job. It can be very gratifying. Remember, you are inspirational by your very own actions. Keep in mind the power you possess and use it wisely.

People—
From My Point of View

S OME PEOPLE DO AND SOME PEOPLE DON'T. Some
people will and some people won't. Some people have feelings but some have none. How one person relates to another
depends on his feelings. Thus, some people can make a person feel good whereas other people really send no message at
all. People are sensitive to most situations that concern them.
Maybe that is why different people react in different ways to
similar situations. Some people have drive. Some have no
idea of what drive really is. Every one of you knows people of
each description.

A lot of what people learned growing up affects them later in
life. The people you meet in school, may have a lifetime effect
on you, just as you may have on them. People are what makes
life interesting. Life needs people to carry it out. Your own life
would be awfully dull without the input of other people
around you. Yet there are many times when people like being
alone. Solitude is the best environment for absorbing the
many feelings that go through people as they live their lives.

I personally like being around people with a positive outlook on life. It takes an upbeat person to have a positive outlook on life. Certain people serve as role models for others.
This is a good thing. When you see that someone else can do
something successfully, you may believe that you might be
able to do the same. When your role models are optimistic,

proactive people, you can set your sights high. This helps in realizing your greatest desires. There should be no limit to success a person hopes to achieve. The world is open to dreamers.

FOR A DREAM TO COME TRUE, YOU MUST WANT IT STRONGLY ENOUGH TO MAKE IT A REALITY.

In life, it is other people who give you gratification. Nothing can be more stimulating than people and their thoughts. What makes one person interesting is the ideas he puts out on the table to think about and discuss. If you don't agree with his ideas, it makes for interesting conversation. Even if you have the same idea or feelings, there's the good feeling that you are not alone. People were meant to be together with other people.

People everywhere are concerned that they count as individuals. They want to be a part of something in their dally lives, whether it be a family, a business or a community, This affiliation with others is essential to life. The people around us make the difference in our lives. We will be influenced, convinced and be sold on any number of things because of the people surrounding us.

Remember, people's views of others are in the eyes of the beholder. These decisions about whether to like or dislike another are made on a continuing basis. It's funny, though, when you think about it, most people see others the same way you do. No one ever really fools anyone. Be true to yourself and you will be true to others and accepted by society more readily

This is a people world so, in a world of people, you really do count.

Fast Track to Success

THE COUNTRY is going through a revolution, as far as the job market is concerned. This has caused much hardship on families, due to the fact that what was once a sure thing is now a big gamble. A person with a family who has worked hard in his career, keeping up his skills, may suddenly find himself out-of-date, redundant, out of a job.

In my community, we realized that people were taking low-paying jobs just to support their families. The professions for which they had prepared were no longer in demand. They were determined to meet their responsibilities, no matter how long and hard they had to work. To help these people, my community put into action an idea they truly believed in. *Success Track*, which offered computer training while simultaneously offering courses in budgeting, preparation of financial statements and writing a business plan.

Part of the program's magic is that the people who taught in it (Joseph Harari, Ted J. Beyda, Harry Ashkenazi, Hurdle Tawil and Ricky Cohen) were successful businessmen who used professional materials in their classes. The demand for the courses was greater than our resources, so we launched a campaign, sending out flyers to synagogues letting people know about the program.

People were pleased to hear that there was a place in the community where people could go to catch up and keep up with today's competitive workplace. Many people came through with contributions to expand the program. In today's fast-moving business climate, even the most well-established businessmen are forced to develop new skills to survive. If a person is going to control his financial future, he needs to learn these skills.

There are three groups of people who benefit from this program: (1) 40–60 year-olds who need retraining; (2) 15–17 year-olds who are completely unaware of the opportunities available to them; and (3) 18–35 year-olds who are seeking employment in the business world. The courses are complemented by Executive Connection, an employment bureau that carries listings for high salaried positions in companies. As Rabbi Michael Haber says, "This is the highest level of charity: helping a person get a job or giving a person the skills to earn an income."

As this program proves, success is a choice. We can go forward as individuals and and as a community with optimism if we choose education. Parents should encourage their children to continue their educations after high school wherever possible. If they believe in the idea of education themselves, their children will feel confident to go on learning throughout life. Programs like *Success Track* make this life-long learning possible.

Mother Nature gives and takes.
Being natural and down to earth
brings reality into focus.

PART THREE
Nature and Human Nature

Summertime

I'T'S SUMMERTIME AND NATURE IS AT HER BEST. The birds and the bees are busier than ever. And so are you young adults who presumably are preparing for the mating season once again. The parties will soon begin, and last however late. You may meet a mate and make a date and for sure you won't be late.

So as the parties start, I look around to get a feel for the new faces. Young adulthood is such a special time in the human life that it is almost make-believe. You are still single. Being free gives you a kind of a tingle. Maybe your heart pounds for a certain someone who makes you ask yourself, can this be happening to me? You will definitely know when the chemistry is right. When the right person seemingly lights up your life. Certainty is the sign you are looking for.

As you converse with one another and get to know each other better, the challenge of one another is the magnet that pulls you together. To take the pressure off, just try being yourself and make the most of the short summer.

Begin with a plan for your summer weekend. Getting together on Friday night with the family is the right way to begin. You are most comfortable with your own family. This gets you relaxed as the weekend begins and the fresh summer ocean air goes through you.

Real talent goes into cooking the Friday night dinner. Then you have all weekend to work it off. We can swim, golf, play tennis and hike across the dunes over the weekend—all sorts of outdoor exercise. But as you look forward to the gatherings at the beaches and pools, and the sunshine to go with it, be sure to use the sun block.

You'll also want to make the most of your summer weekends by taking care not to drink and drive, not only for your safety, but for the safety of your friends and others around you. Pay attention to the speed limit wherever you are. Don't double park to have a conversation anywhere. It's just plain inconsiderate and not safe.

Now that I've laid down some rules for getting the most out of the summer, let me wish you all a wonderful season that will fill you with sunshine and smiles-lots of smiles. To be young in this spectacular season is a reason for laughing, so try not to be too serious. Laughter helps to make you feel more at ease in the bold light of the summer sun.

Nature, Central Park Style

THE SWEET SMELL OF SUCCESS comes when spring blossoms permeate the air. Having gone through a most severe winter, you now have the opportunity to appreciate the things that nature has to offer in the spring. A walk through Central Park at lunchtime will let you witness the freedom of nature. The bright green grass is growing in, after lying dormant all winter. The elms, the maples, the lindens and oaks are beginning to sprout their leaves once again. As you watch them grow from week to week, they are like a new-born baby growing stronger and bigger each day.

As you walk by the lake, you see ducks in many colors floating on the water. The water can also be appreciated for the many images it reflects, the beautiful boathouse, the crags and the flowers. You see children being rolled in their strollers, babies in their carriages. People of all ages are strolling, walking, jogging and running through the park.

Wollman Rink used for ice skating all winter, is now a place for roller skates and roller blades. What a pretty sight! Along the transverses, some cyclists go at their own pace, while others pedal furiously as though it were a race.

Every spring, I like a seat on a park bench to kind of catch up with all that is going on.

The horse-drawn carriages move along with their picturesque passengers—people from every country imaginable, from states far and wide, lovers, businessmen, children—people who have never been to our beautiful Central Park before. Beyond the Great Lawn lie the ball fields, where many games are being played. The red clay around the green grass doffed with the white bases indicates a good time in the sunshine from above, with a sparse cloud or two to paint a picture that nature provides us to enjoy.

As Spring rolls into summer, be careful to enjoy the sun under a shady tree, with some sun block to protect you from the rays. Sight a rainbow or smell the grass after a refreshing thunderstorm. Enjoy the good side of nature by remembering how short spring is in New York City. As I watch Nature on a grand scale in Central Park, I think of working in my garden, teaching my grandsons about the earth and its riches. Here in eighty acres in the middle of the greatest city in the world, I watch the miracle of Spring starting a new cycle of seed time and harvest. Appreciate nature and you will appreciate more of what life has to offer. Just let the sun shine in your heart and your moods will be brighter, your feelings will be lighter.

Understanding Yourself

UNDERSTANDING YOURSELF IS NO EASY TASK. The things that affect you can be complex. There are many different reasons for responding to certain events. Some things make one person feel terrible, while they may have no effect on the next person. What bothers you may bother you and you alone.

The first thing to realize is that everyone is made of the same stuff. Every human being has similar feelings, likes and dislikes. This is not to say that all people share the same views on any given subject! Each individual has his own ways of reacting to things. That's what creates individuality.

Make a list of the things that happened to you during the course of the day. Trying to be a better person for the sake of yourself should really be your goal. By reflecting on your day, you may accomplish your aims. All human beings find gratification and happiness by doing good and helping others.

A rabbi recently told me that he can only eat one meal at a time. How much does he really need? How much does any man really need? How much is too much? This rabbi knows that carrying materialism too far can get the best of any individual. Material things are nice, but they shouldn't rule your life. You can protect yourself from the tyranny of materialism by going back to basics. Make things simple.

Society has a definite influence on us. It is up to you as an individual to set the priorities that govern your life. How do you as an individual set your priorities? What is the level of importance that you put on things and how do they affect you in the long run?

To my way of thinking, family means a lot. In order of importance in my life, it is first and foremost. I feel it is my responsibility as a family man to teach real values to my children and grandchildren. Giving without good reason has little impact. In today's society the tendency is to give children the things the parents and grandparents didn't have when they were growing up. Well and good, but this may not be the best thing for the children. Be careful not to indulge children in excess. If everything is given to them too readily when they are young, they will have unrealistic expectations when they reach adulthood. A child who has been over-indulged may expect the world to take care of him. He will find it hard to adjust to the realities of life. Essential to living realistically in adulthood is having an education and knowing a trade. This is what parents should be giving to children. It has been shown that people with a college education have a definite advantage over those who haven't had one.

Knowledge is like food. Without knowledge, people do not move forward. You want to give knowledge to yourself as well as to your children. Giving yourself every opportunity to get more education at any age will give you an opportunity to be successful economically and socially.

Keeping life simple by setting your priorities will help you better understand yourselves. Try saying "hello" to someone else before they say "hello" to you first. This would be a good first step to feeling good about yourself. Get to know yourself and you will get to know others. Keep smiling and have a great day!

Memories

FORWARD MOTION is a natural instinct in a human being. So it is that everything follows suit, including the mind. I was reminded of this by a recent conversation I had with a long-time friend whom I see from time to time.

I was very moved by what I had heard from him. Here was a man in his late sixties who felt he never had any break in life. He had worked hard all his life to support his family, which he has done successfully. We got into a discussion about our children. Was it right to hit them as punishment when they misbehaved, as they were growing up?

He has three daughters and recalled how he hit one of his daughters when she came home very late from a date. She was only about sixteen at the time. He told me that the relationship was never the same after that. It was the only time he had ever hit any of his children. He was very upset by the memory of the incident and almost broke down and cried as he told me the story. It was something that was still bothering him a good twenty years after the incident.

It's often good to analyze and think about life from both sides. The side that makes you feel good and the side that says, why did I do a certain thing this way instead of that way? The reason for analysis is to try to refine our thoughts and our reactions to them in the future. Yet it's important to remember that when you reflect on the past, you should try not to let it negatively affect you.

The only material thing you can learn from things that went wrong in the past is how to improve your attitude in the future. Living in the past, hating yourself for what is water under the bridge is pointless. Many people live in the past, to no avail. The past is a tool for the future not a goal in itself.

I have a way of controlling negative feelings for the moment by saying to myself: "How will I feel about what happened a week from now, a month from now, and a year from now?"

In most cases, you won't even remember things you thought of as glaring incidents. They won't even be meaningful a week or two later. Time has a way of healing most feelings. To look back in time it is medicinal to remember the good times as well as the bad ones. You can learn from positive experiences as well as negative ones. Recall the good people who were around you as well as your enemies to look out for. Why let things get you down? In the long run, past events will have a limited meaning in the overall picture of your life.

Everything that happens has a good side to it. Just look at how much you learn from a mistake. If you don't make mistakes, you will never learn. Education and experience both have a cost. If you do nothing you will never make a mistake, but what will you have learned and achieved? Live and learn, but never forget to go with the forward flow that makes life worth living.

Happiness

WHAT HAVE YOU BEEN DOING LATELY? Does it make you feel happy? People don't necessarily go out of their way to make happiness happen. Life can be pretty dull at times. Winter storms can really make people feel low. Summer heat can really get people down. Stuck in the house because it's too hot or too cold or too wet or too icy can make a person unhappy under the best of circumstances.

Life is like that too. My theory is that if you are stuck, you have to get yourself out. No matter how bad the situation around you is, you can find a way to find happiness. The first thing I authorize is change. Not loose change. Real change. Change for the better. Stuck in the house on a stormy weekend? Read a book, catch up on the newspaper, or study the

Bible. These are the kind of things that will get your emotions going.

You can also discuss proverbs and play games to get the mind going. For the body to be refreshed, it needs oxygen. This means activity. Mental aerobics can be as stimulating as a workout in the gym. A teacher one time asked the class for a definition of happiness, so I raised my hand. I said that happiness is the culmination of something that has been building up over a period of time. That definition still works for me.

To be happy about something you really have to earn it. The best example I can give is when trying to crack open a big account. After months of making phone calls I finally get the buyer on the phone. This is stage one. Stage two is getting a positive reaction, like an appointment with the buyer. Stage three is getting the first order. To me, as a salesman, this is the height of happiness. I went after something and I got it. I worked for it and it worked for me.

You can seek happiness in your own situation in the same way. You set a goal, you keep your eye on the next step. Once you achieve step one, you move on to step two. And step two leads you to step three—and happiness! This can work even when you are getting ready for a vacation. Just planning it is exciting. You take it to step two, setting out. Then step three—being there. The vacation itself is a short time and before you know it you're back home. But you planned and worked for a good time. The vacation made you happy.

In sales, in vacations and throughout life, it's the people you work with and play with who make your experiences happy. The customer is pleased because he's having success with what you sold him. Your children are pleased because they loved being at the beach where you took them for summer vacation. Most relationships these days are short and sweet. But when we meet, there is a chance for happiness. Wherever you are, try being consciously happy about something good you have done for someone in your life. It will exhilarate you at the very least.

Happiness is a state of mind. Every day you are in a different state. So keep moving forward. As long as you work for it, it's never too late for happiness.

P.S.—Try putting a picture of someone you love with a big smile on your desk or in your kitchen. Guaranteed to make you smile every time you look at it!

Learning By Observing

THE ADVANTAGES SOME PEOPLE have over others is that they have a natural talent to learn and grow by observing others. Many people have the opportunity to learn just by watching and remembering but do not recognize the opportunity. As the years go by, you will come into contact with many people in many different situations.

You will probably find that you react to the way other people speak and handle themselves. This is natural. It is important for you to register your emotions as you watch other people. This will be your signal if there is anything worth learning from that other person.

If his behavior has had an impact on you, you will keep the impression he made on you. Naturally you may not agree with what the other person had done or said, but it is important for you to realize that you have learned something. People continually learn from others. The point is that people learn what is right as well as what is not right by observing and assessing the words and actions of others. In every situation, you will see many different kinds of behavior. It's up to you to choose the one that works for you.

It is up to you to realize that you will be molding your character and personality as you learn the right thing to do from others around you. Analysis of everything and everyone around you can be learned by training yourself to observe things. Look around yourself regularly. It will be to your advantage, especially when it comes to being able to handle other people. You can learn from people who are diplomatic as you watch their negotiation professionally. You can also learn what not to do from people who blow up the instant they don't get their own way. You must strive to learn from the best, to reject the worst in order to achieve the best results you can.

When playing golf for example, many things can be learned by observing. When putting, if someone putts before you that has the same line of direction, you can see the way the other player's ball rolls towards the hole to better your chances to sink the ball when it is your turn.

When you are raising children, you are being quietly observed by your youngsters. They do more learning from parents than anyone realizes. That is why it is necessary for parents to understand what powerful role models they are. It doesn't stop with childhood either—children use their parents for role models all the way through retirement! So don't think that just because you are getting older, you know enough and stop learning. That's not how the human being is. The human hunger for learning never stops. It actually grows as people go through life. Observing others around us gives us ideas that nourish our minds.

As important as remembering the good things you learn from others is filtering out the bad things. It is a fact that 75% of the time people spend listening to others; yet people retain only 20% to 25% of what they hear. People do a lot of filtering to try to make room for the good things that are important to remember.

Take the time to concentrate and observe others as a learning experience. Learning to listen to others is a big advantage in learning and growing. Show that you are interested in what the next person has to say-and the next person will also be patient to hear what you have to say. You will, at the same time, have the opportunity to observe and maybe learn something refreshing.

Now you are on your own. So good luck with the earnings you will gain from learning by listening and observing.

Adolescence

EVERYONE UNDERGOES ADOLESCENCE, but each person experiences it differently. This rite of passage is uniquely your own. Nonetheless, there will be some experiences in this time of your life that you will share with others. For instance, the time you live in plays a major part in the way you think about becoming an adult. Depending on what is happening in the world—the Depression of the 30's, the upheaval of the 60s or the prosperity of the 90s—each period of adolescence is shared by those who are young. The factors of the times play a role in how serious about life we were as we grew up from the ages of thirteen to twenty.

For my generation, the draft law that was in effect for a hundred years until 1972 played a big part. Serving in the armed forces for two years was something every young man had to do. This service was done right after high school prior to going out into the world and getting a job.

For today's generation of teenagers, there is more pressure than ever. There are several reasons for this phenomenon. Teenagers of today are more knowledgeable than ever before. Their skill with computers is a feat their adults would never have dreamed could be possible in their lifetime. Their physical fitness, their awareness of world events and their ambitions to make the world a better place are awesome. Yet they have problems: the pressure for teenagers to get along with others is great. The competition to excel is even greater. Parents have a hard time advising young people because they didn't grow up with these pressures. Studying the needs of today's adolescents is essential for parents who want to play an important role in their children's teenage development.

Teaching your children early on, and staying with them as they develop is the best preparation for communication when they reach adolescence. Parents should consider various ways to instill values into their children as early as possible. Rewarding a child for something productive she has done is one way to teach her good values.

Giving in to adolescents is very easy. Teenagers will always be testing you. It is up to you as the parent to realize that you will pay the price for conceding.

Teach your child the meaning of a dollar in a way the child can understand. Let respect for one another rule over everything. Let manners dictate the order of the day. This is only part of the recipe for giving your youngster real values they can take through life. The lessons you teach will cushion their way through adolescence. More importantly, they will impart this wisdom to their children as they set out to raise a family.

The parent who does not allot time for raising the child should expect to have a child who will go his own way. Maintaining a working relationship with your child is no different than maintaining one with others in your life. Don't treat it any differently. And don't let it slip away when your child reaches adolescence. By speaking to teenagers you can find out what their needs are. They are quite different than yours were because we are living in a time of prosperity and stiff competition. Take the time to help them through the transition from childhood to adulthood. Show your teenager that you care enough to work it out with him.

Retirement

PART I

As THE YEARS PASS, and I get older, I have begun to think about retirement and what it means to me. Most people are very active during their working years. However when that part of your life ends, you must begin to think of new ways to stay active, healthy, and young at heart. This means exercising your body and mind. The mind is like every other part of the body. It needs nourishment to keep sharp and focused. One way to do this is to reflect on your life experiences or create a family tree. Try sitting down to write about some of the highlights in your life. With regards to the body, hobbies can play an important role. I have managed to develop several hobbies over the years. Gardening is one which gives me good exercise and gratification. Golf is also a fun way to get some exercise, and meet new people on the course. Community service is also a great way to fill your time and give you a real sense of accomplishment.

I had a conversation with my local family doctor recently and he felt that he would not recommend retirement to anyone. He is in his late sixties, and admits that he is slowing down, but that comes with aging. I personally feel that retirement is not for everyone. Recently I went walking on Ocean Avenue in Long Branch one nice sunny day to get some exercise. As I walked, I met an old friend of my father's. We began talking, and I asked him what he was doing these days. He replied that he had retired a couple of years ago. I asked him, "What made you retire?" He said that at eighty eight years of age he had just got tired. I had to laugh to myself because I understood what he meant. It was a very good reason.

Things can get boring at times. That is why it is important to develop your skills as you go through life. The way I look at it, a person should keep as active as possible with or without retirement. Life can be very fulfilling, especially when doing the things you like to do. But only you can define that.

I do business with Mr. Elmer Kaplin and his son Ned who are from Philadelphia. Elmer is the founder of a company called House of Bargains. Ned runs the business and is very active. His father goes to Florida during the winter months and stays up north during the rest of the year. Mr. Kaplin fought in World War II and was among the first troops to free survivors in the death camps. I asked him if he would write an article concerning his feelings about retirement. The following is his perspective on retirement.

Retirement

PART II

by Elmer Kaplin

I AM 83 YEARS OLD and still a little active in our business. At my age, I am not capable of doing all the things that a younger man could do, but I do what I can. Going to work gives me an incentive to get up in the morning. A good many of my friends sleep late everyday. But I know that people are counting on me, and that is all the motivation I need.

In the winter, I go to Florida. It can become very boring down there. Often, there is nothing to do except play golf and worry about where to eat at night. To break up the monotony, I like to fly up north to help with the business. About every three to four weeks I will spend four or five days doing some work. It invigorates me and helps me enjoy my vacation down south a little more.

The only people who should retire are those who have hobbies that will keep them busy. Some of my friends are artists, some love to work with their hands. They make use of their retirement. If a person does not have something to keep him busy he will wither on the vine.

Retirement

PART III

IN CLOSING, I WOULD AGREE with Mr Kaplin's thoughts about retirement. I think that he is right on the money. Keep young and energetic by exercising and having a positive outlook on life.

Rabbi Saul Kassin told me that the more he studies, the more he realizes how much more he still has to learn. This to me, is the definition of a young outlook on life. Never believe that the world doesn't have something new and different for you to discover.

I hope the people that I have spoken about are a good example to help you get a jump on retirement.

May the sun shine for you with bright ideas every day. And oh yes—keep smiling.

Life and Time

WE REALLY LIVE OUR DAILY LIVES in a very simple way. Individually, each member of the family is a participant of the activities that flow around a family.

I guess you could say that we are a family team. Everyone's function is important. Sometimes, we tend to get lost in the shuffle of time. Time happens to be our most precious asset. What we do with it creates the value. This is mostly dictated by the way we run our lives.

First of all, we must sleep for about eight hours for our bodies to carry out the many actions of the day. That leaves us about sixteen hours to slice the day with.

We travel to and from school, work, etc. We eat three meals a day. We need some time for recreation, like reading the paper, or maybe sitting around after dinner with the family to discuss the days activities.

This does not include the hours spent at work or in school. Work hours are dictated by the type of job you have. Homework after school depends on how much work the teacher gave you and how dedicated you are to succeed.

In the final analysis, time can go by very fast, depending on how active you are. Things can really be dull when time goes too slowly, not that I am in a rush. I find that for the time to go at a decent pace, I must be very involved in my daily projects. You must make your job interesting. If you find that what you do is not interesting enough for you, it is up to you to find your way through life and to be happy at what you do.

This is only a day that we have spoken about. Enough said for the present. Now let's look a the future. Isn't it amazing how the years pass by and very little seems to change? Time goes by as we push forward.

All we can really do is look back and say what have we accomplished in our lives? What can we expect to accomplish going forward?

Just some words of advice. Try not to complicate your thoughts. Try thinking in straight lines. Ask your self what are the pluses and minuses of what you choose to do. What will the outlook most likely be. It is up to us to set our goals daily so that life will go forward as it should.

Life is really very simple. There isn't that much that we have to say about it. We are really driven by the forces around us-that is once we have chosen our future. It sure gives you a lot to think about

Having an Open Mind

THROUGH THE COURSE OF THE DAY, I have many conversations with many different kinds of people. Some of what I hear, I agree with, some I do not. But even if you don't believe everything you hear, it is important to have an open mind about other peoples thoughts and opinions.

By keeping an open mind, you are giving yourself a greater opportunity to learn. By listening instead of dismissing what other people have to say, you can better understand their ideas. In many cases both parties can be turned off from one another because they hear, but are not really listening.

Parent and child relationships fit this situation. If a parent doesn't listen to a child's side of the story, that parent is unconsciously telling that child that nothing they have to say is important. As a parent, it is your responsibility to encourage your children, and make them feel confident in themselves. You are also teaching them important ground rules for life. They must learn to think before speaking, but to speak when they have something to say. It also shows them, by example, to listen to the other side patiently, and wait their turn to talk. It is good to be firm with children and not be afraid to say no to them. But tell them why you made a particular decision, even if they don't seem to understand or care at the time. They are listening, and will respect your decisions later on, if they know that you have employed logic and reason, and taken the time to explain it to them.

There are many advantages to keeping an open mind. It gives a person some satisfaction to know that you are listening to what they have to say. It also adds a positive influence to the conversation. It means that by giving a little, you get a lot. By not prejudging other people's ideas, you are heightening the chance that they will listen respectfully to you.

When having a conversation with others, listen with open ears and an open mind. Think of it as a window of opportunity. We can learn from everyone. From some people I have even learned about what not to do. If you keep an open mind, you will increase your chances for success.

Good Luck.

Going Off the Deep End

W E DEAL WITH MANY EXTREMES IN LIFE. One extreme that we all come into contact with is the weather. The weather can change from hot and sunny, to cloudy and rainy so quickly. A real extreme for me is the winter. In the winter the weather can be brisk and sunny one day, and icy and windy the next. These are all examples of extremes in nature. Even the weatherman can not always predict what will happen tomorrow. The weather is one of many things that we as humans, just can't control.

Something that people often try to control, sometimes successfully sometimes not, is their own human nature. An obvious example that comes to mind is weight control. Everyone seems to go up and down the scale. Yo-yo diets are difficult to keep up with. More up than down, we keep the scales of hope pretty busy. Going on a healthy diet and losing weight is the obvious ideal. But why is it that dieters often fall short of their goal? Everyone loves good food. One "taste" is worth a thousand words—or is it calories?

Perhaps the problem is in the method. Extremes can be exciting but the Golden Mean remains, moderation. Feast or famine should not be a necessary function of life. In fact, formulating good eating should be a necessary function. Instead of eating a lot one day, and then trying to make it up the next, try eating a little less each meal. I know that moderation can be tough. I have the most difficulty at Friday night dinner with the family. But remember, most everything you do is or will become, habit. By realizing that you create your own habits, you can learn to change them for the better. Instead of going off the deep end, try creating some sort of equilibrium in your eating habits.

Eating isn't the only thing that requires moderation. Extremes and going off the deep end threaten everything you do. It threatens your sense of reality, your stability and your comfort. Without moderation, no one could succeed for very long. So try and find the perfect middle which keeps you happy and gives you a little control in a sometimes crazy world!

Thoughts on Caring

WHEN YOU TAKE THE TIME to care about other people and their feelings, they will usually return the compliment.

Caring is more than just being nice to someone, it also means helping them even if it is inconvenient to you, and thinking of them even if they are not there physically to remind you.

Don't be afraid to make the first move, showing that you care about someone is the first step in a very rewarding process.

Do what is in your heart, and you will never regret it.

When it comes to family, friends, business associates, and acquaintances, try to be helpful. Share what you know with others, caring about people means giving them advice when they need it.

If you give to your community, what you receive in return is priceless.

Always share the spotlight and the work. If you care about the members of your team, you will get along better, and will have a better chance at success.

Carry a little extra happiness with you, wherever you go, and give it to whoever needs it most. If you make the effort to make others happy, they will always be grateful and want to be near you.

Don't lose sight of yourself when you go out into the world. Keep your identity, remember that you are unique and special in your own way. And if you don't lose sight of it, you can do something extraordinary with your life.

If you stop thinking of what you can receive, and start thinking of what you can give, your true creative nature will come forth to help you, and you will be surprised at what will follow.

Never forget that love is the most important gift we have been given, but if you are too focused on yourself, you may miss your chance.

A marriage will surely last when each partner has a true caring for the other's feelings and needs.

The first step in marriage is to discover all the treasures of the other person's self, the second step is to share those treasures with your children.

Step three is getting them through school and teaching them that simple emotions such as love and caring still exist in this fast-paced, digital world.

Before you know it your children will be all grown up and starting families of their own, so always show them that you love them, and teach them to love others.

P.S.—True caring (love and feelings) comes from the heart.

History Repeats Itself

HISTORY IS REALLY A STORY OF THE PAST. Learning from history is how man betters himself. In life, as the saying goes, history repeats itself. People are inclined to do the things they have seen their parents do. Each generation is almost a clone of previous generations. The only change that I have noticed in my lifetime is that in modern times, things happen a lot faster. The perspective may be a little different because of the speed of life these days.

Well, depending on who you are, you might be able to see some of the weaknesses that prior generations have passed on to you. While it is easy to see that politics, war and greed persist, it's harder to see that your generation hasn't changed much from your parents' generation. Human tendencies have not gone away nor have they changed much. Unfortunately, people still seek power.

Change does not come easily. People are creatures of habit. And there is no point in changing just for the sake of change. But sometimes a change can be a good idea. If you can see that a small thing, like doing good deeds more often, that makes a change from the previous generation, you should do it. It makes you feel better about yourself, and you know that you are improving. It's up to you to learn from life's experiences. By setting a good example to people your age, you offer an alternative to the enduring human qualities of greed, war and politics. You become an example that helps others learn and improve on what they already know.

Yet there are many things that you can learn from the previous generations. Giving respect to them at all times is something to think about. No one can know everything and no one can know enough. As I grow older I realize how much there is to know and learn. Even at my age, I look to the previous generation for help and wisdom. This only tells me how little I really know.

Never stop learning from history, because it is from history that mankind builds a better world.

The Nature of Retailing

RECENT NEWSPAPER AND TELEVISION COVERAGE has created alarm in the retailing community by showing the demise of great retail giants. Arnold Constable, which recently closed, had been around the New York City scene since the 1820s. It's just one of the many stores that have disappeared. In the past thirty years, fifteen department stores have ceased to exist. Many of the original discounters of the 1960's like Korvettes have disappeared. What has caused all this to happen? You could probably say that these retailers have failed to keep up with changing times.

The way I see it, the retailing competition is a lot keener than it has been. Newer, bigger, more competitive operations such as Sam Walton's Walmart have come on the scene, forcing the competition to look up and take notice.

The department store has quietly become an advertising discounter. It has been a very successful strategy. The mom-and-pop stores are becoming a thing of the past. They are just not strong enough to survive against the retailing giants. Small chains are merging because it's either merge—or disappear!

The category killers have big muscle. Toys "Я" Us® is one example, opening stores all over the world in order to expand their volume.

What will the future bring in retailing? I can say, as someone who has spent 46 years in the business, that competition will increase. Any store that wants to survive has to keep operating costs down to the bone. Low operating costs are required not only to show good profits, but to exist at all.

We have a surplus of stores and not enough customers to go around. The result is that when it comes to getting good value, the retailer's first job is to get the customer to his store. Then he has to offer good value. Right now, the retail customer will continue to have the upper hand. The retail scene today is one where only the fittest will survive.

Having a sense of value
of all the things around you
will bring good thoughts together.

PART FOUR

Putting it All Together

True Values

WHEN YOU THINK ABOUT THE THINGS THAT YOU DO, are you able to weigh your true value?

When you see the people around you during the course of a day, are you able to weigh their true value?

How do you value the quality of life that you have, and what you have achieved? To be happy with yourself it is important to understand the true value of life and all that is around you, regularly. Who are we trying to impress and why, are questions for you to answer.

Be down to earth with yourself. It is a good way to start; being realistic and true to one's self are both traits that are admired by others.

A person must believe in himself and have the confidence to be able to inspire others in a positive way. In the same way, you are improving your quality of life and creating a true value.

To me, the true value of life is how you enjoy people and nature, which has two meanings: "real life" and "still life." The former regards your daily interactions with others. Value the little things that your friends, family, and even strangers do for you to get the most out of your life.

"Still life" has to do with art, nature, and culture. When was the last time you visited the Metropolitan Museum of Art, for example? Learn to value these cultural commodities. This will enhance your still life.

Spend time appreciating your family by enjoying precious moments with your children and grandchildren. Having dinner with your parents and grandparents can create a feeling that builds strong family values.

Showing care and love and being thoughtful towards one another are the building blocks that will create a true value within yourself and those around you.

How do you value your community? I see a community that has been built over a number of decades. Having lived through much of the changes that have occurred during this period of time, I can truly say "Wow!" I realize that it did not just happen. It took very special people to have the foresight and the guts to make necessary decisions for us to move forward. These people gave us all a true value. I am really amazed at how a community working together like a family can accomplish so much!

Give worth to everything you do; and you will have the satisfaction of accomplishment in whatever you do.

Understanding the value of a good family, a good friend and a good job will increase true value of one's life. As the saying goes, smile and the whole world smiles with you. Being you is more important than anything else because you are an individual and very special at that.

So, get your money's worth everyday and don't short change yourself. Appreciate what you have and you will have a true value for all your lifetime.

Feelings

HAVE YOU EVER TOUCHED SOMEONE without physically touching them? Did you ever get the feeling that you were moved without ever being touched? The magical sense that can move us, is the sense of feeling. As I write you now, I have the feeling to do so, or I would probably not want to do it. Get those juices flowing. Create competition for yourself. Search your inner self as to what you experience for the moment.

I love to laugh and smile. It makes me feel good. It's also good to make other people feel good about themselves. Being yourself and being what I call natural creates a warm feeling. No one is hang-up free, and no one is perfect. Just be loose as a goose and believe me, life will be a lot easier

Your reflection of attitude is most important to the success in ones life. How you come off to the next person can mean the difference in success in your life. A smile and some kind words are very meaningful to others as well. Good feelings can make the difference in the outcome of your day. Try making someone feel good with a simple smile.

Remember, it is up to you to make yourself feel good. Think about it. When you smile at someone they will most likely smile back at you. At the same time you both react in kind.

So keep on smiling and feeling good until we meet again.

P.S.—If after reading the above you have been touched but not physically, you might say you have been moved by your feelings.

Times Have Changed

GOING BACK MANY YEARS, I remember when I first started working full time. Times were different in the mid 1950's. Eisenhower was president. People were pretty conservative. There was a war going on in Korea and the draft was a threat to most young men. I remember trying to join the National Guard at that time. When I was rejected, I turned to my family for help. That's how I began working in the family business.

We would work six days a week. Leave at six A.M. and be ready for work 45 minutes later. It was a long day. You were on your feet all day, stopping briefly to have a cream cheese sandwich. By the time we returned back home it was 8:30 P.M. Mom would be waiting to serve us dinner. Sometimes we watched a little T.V. but usually I was so tired I went to bed very soon after.

In those days you did like everyone else in the family did. The routine was always the same. The heads of the family ran your life and that's the way it was. Today, things are a little different. People are not as easily satisfied as they were back then. Children are more independent, they have their own dreams, and they want to find their own paths. Since people today want a better quality of life, the pressure to succeed is far greater. Kids today must also learn to be competitive at an earlier age. Many children go to private schools, especially in religious communities.

All these changes cause more strain on parents as well. They must find a way to give their children what they will need to get ahead in this competitive, fast paced world. It is up to them to guide their children, and give them the strength and competence to find their own path amongst their peers. The dynamics of the family have changed as well. Young married people today have a greater sense of responsibility to one another. They split household duties more equally. And must work harder to keep the lines of communication open. When the family grows, both the husband and wife take active roles in the parenting.

Here we are in the 90's and the newest revolution since T.V. is making its way into the home of the American family. Computers have become a big part of our lives, in the work place, and in the family. They educate and entertain children. With yet another instrument to make life easier and faster, it is up to you to prioritize your time. You need to balance work and family so that your children won't be staring at screens more than anything else. And sometimes, if you spend too much time trying to cut corners, you will miss out on things that could be important for you to experience.

Balance is the key, in parenting, business, and life. Learn hobbies and play sports with your children. Take advantage of modern technology to make your life better, not worse. And don't forget that there is more to life than just what you are experiencing. It is a big world out there, your life is just one addition to a far greater whole. Keep smiling at home and at work and you will make your life extraordinary.

The Rewards Of Life

I RECENTLY ATTENDED a B'nai B'rith dinner honoring a woman that has been an inspiration of monumental proportions to children all over the world. Her face may not be pasted on billboards, but she has been a great addition to the world of imagination and youth. Her name is Sheryl Leach. She is the creator of Barney, the purple dinosaur.

It was a very entertaining evening. The speakers were interesting and informative. My son was supposed to say a few words, but couldn't stay. He was on his way to Chicago to plug some Barney sales. So I pinched hit for him.

After I read the part my son had given me to read, I stuck in a few of my own words. I finished by telling Sheryl she is as rare as the dinosaur she created. Of course, she is not extinct. But she really brought the dinosaur, which is extinct, back to life for children everywhere. May she continue to bring her constituency much happiness. I can STILL hear the laughter.

I think that the most important thing I took home with me that evening is the knowledge that participation is the key to life. Getting involved and being a part of something productive that can help others is self rewarding. Your kindness can have a direct effect on someone else.

Many of the people in my community meet the challenge of self-reward daily. They have the opportunity to do so because of the many institutions that serve my community. It is these kind of people that help to shape and form the character of a community. It is only through the hard work and dedication of these few, that people will take notice, and give back to their community.

Several years ago I started writing to the Deal Community from my synagogue every week during the summer months. I would mail out a copy to about fifteen hundred families. It would take me three to four hours on a Sunday to put the letter together. Then it would be typed on Monday, proof read and then sent off to the printer. It would arrive in homes just in time for Friday night reading with the family.

It lasted for about four years and was very successful. When I stopped, people asked me to continue writing. That was when I decided to write for the *Image Magazine.* Not knowing what I would write about, it just kind of developed. The theme behind my writing has always been to try to help others through my experience in life. I have explained all this to you to show you how much gratification and positive feedback you can get by being involved in community work in some way.

It is up to you to set some time aside to give back what you have learned about life. We are all messengers of one kind or another and it is up to us as individuals to deliver it. I take this opportunity to thank you, the reader, and implore you to be a part of the leadership that has helped my community grow to such heights.

Don't take anything for granted. Young ones must be given the opportunity to learn and continue on, to carry the torch of kindness and caring. Just like Sheryl Leach had an idea to help mankind, so can you. She is a real inspiration to me, as well as the kids that know Barney all over the world.

Responsibility

THE GREATEST gift you can give a child is responsibility. It is one thing that they will have throughout their lives. Material things and money can never last that long. Try giving your child the right to do and think for themselves, and be treated like adults early on. You can start by giving your child limited responsibilities, and then follow up to make sure they have been completed.

Responsibility is like fiber. A necessary ingredient for our bodies. It helps a young body to grow strong and answers the many questions our young ones have when they reach high school and even college. Today I find that so many high school and college students are lost in many ways. They need direction. They look to others for advice and encouragement. You have the responsibility of listening to what this new generation has to say, and guiding them to the truth. They will be responsible for their own identities, they will have to find their own way. But you can help them.

Having had the opportunity to speak to a group of college students, I found that they had many thoughts and questions that they needed answers to. But I get the feeling that these young adults might be happier to get answers from people outside of their immediate family. It's a funny thing that parents are often the last person that the child will listen to. And yet many of them are making one of the hardest transitions in life, from dependency to independency.

Many of your children are finishing their final years of schooling and are about to join the working world. Now is the time to make sure they have learned something about responsibility. Because they will be the future leaders. The money is on them to carry the ball. If you never trusted them with anything while they were growing up, how can you expect them to handle the pressure of having coworkers, employers, and significant others depend on them now?

There are no lessons on how to raise a child. It is more a trial and error process, that requires a mixture of instinct, reason, and patience. I'm sure there are books available on the subject. But if you're like most parents, you don't have the time for things like that. But one thing you can do is have the confidence in yourself to have the confidence in your child. Trust them to make the right decisions but also don't be afraid to let them make mistakes. Making mistakes are a big part of learning.

So, until they reach the responsibility of self support, it is up to you as members of your community to assist and encourage the young adults with good advice and continuous reinforcement. With your moral support the youngsters of today will succeed as you have.

Unity

AT THE PHILHARMONIC, there are many instruments playing the same tune at the same time. When one instrument is off- key, it can ruin the sound of the entire orchestra. Each musician must be completely aware of, and in unison with the others. It is only when each musician contributes his own unique sound to the whole, that the music produced is beautiful. This beauty is not just the sum of many unique sounds, but it is the far greater beauty of unity.

Unity is important in your personal life as well. A good example is a marriage or a friendship. It takes many things working together to make it successful. Effort is one very important ingredient, which both parties need to add to the mix. A positive attitude is necessary for things to run smoothly and properly. But what is most important is that each person gives equally and lovingly to the relationship, so that the whole is greater than the sum of its parts.

In business, it takes many years of practice and adjustment, until you succeed and become profitable. All people involved must work together like a finely tuned motor to achieve fulfillment. There are many people involved in a business. Everyone has to be thinking along the same lines for it to succeed. Fresh ideas and much effort will keep the motor going at a steady pace. In order to achieve growth, the goal of everyone involved must be the same.

Community is derived from the word unity. Success is based on the idea that each institution in a community plays a key role in the delicate balance needed for it to succeed. When there is a breakdown, for example, and each institution goes in a different direction, there is a failure, as far as unity goes, and so goes the community.

But each individual must also give a good example to the next generation. The members of a community must continue to improve on their society. Each person must be a part of this regeneration in order for unity to continue. It took many years to get to where you are and to achieve the success you can enjoy today in your community. With a unified outlook and goal, a community can continue to grow in strength, into the next century. On a grander scale, a community must work together in all areas to have unity. The same could be said for a city, whatever the size.

A human being is similar to a clock. He just keeps moving along with time. It's what you make of that time that counts. Let us be responsible to make sure that the present formula continues to work, where all of our institutions will work together like a coordinated orchestra. The message is quite clear. In order for two people to be happy with one another or for people in business to get along together or for a community to succeed as one, they all must be united.

Let the Sun Shine

WHEN THE WARM WEATHER ARRIVES, the heavy clothes of winter are stored away. The trees and flowers are in full bloom. My spirits are higher and I become more comfortable in my loose, light clothes. But the best thing about the warm weather is the sun. When the sun shines I feel blessed for a number of reasons. The sun brightens my feelings and outlook on life. I feel more relaxed and smile with greater ease. It is time to take advantage of all these positive natural changes and look at life with a fresher perspective.

The sun makes me want to be outside, in parks or at the beach. With the beauty of nature all around, my imagination can run free. I can escape my inhibitions and fears. It is then that I can see things with new clarity. I can look at my life, and what it means to me and the people I love.

It is important to see that you are a part of a much larger and more intricate web. If you pull on the strings, it will affect other people as well as yourself. Because of this, you should always think about your actions and their repercussions. It is important to maintain a sense of self which you can use to judge what you do, who you talk to, and where you go. If you remember the thoughts you have had, and maintain a sunny disposition, you can make sure that you have a positive effect on others.

When I am in a synagogue on the Sabbath, it could be cloudy or rainy outside yet the sun shines in for all of us. We are all together in prayer and friendship even beneath those dark skies. It should be the same way in our home and at work as well. Let the sun shine in at all times, with happiness to be with one another. Give of yourself to others with an open heart. Let the rays of sunshine sparkle in your heart. A smile has more value and strength than you might realize.

You eventually come to realize what you really are through self-expression and honesty. Be true to yourself and you will be the beneficiary. Somehow everyone knows when a person is true and honest. Let the sunshine reach into the depths of your heart and allow you to live a more fulfilling life with everyone around you every day.

Simplicity

THERE ARE MANY WAYS to simplify your life. Just look at all the time you waste during each day. Once you see how much time you squander, you will find life is more pleasant, not just for yourself but for those around you.

If you make things too complicated, you will never get all the things done that you mean to get done. Life can be simpler and easier if people stopped wasting energy by making things more complicated than they really are. Step one in the right direction is cutting the middleman out of your life. There are usually a ton of extra steps that are not necessary in our most common routines. Start with your family.

Family life can be simplified if you deal with each member directly. If you depend only on first-hand interactions with your family, you won't have to be annoyed with "he/she said" complications.

Simplicity means getting to the point. Anyone can go around the block to cross the street. But if you are direct in your actions, you will get across the street before anyone else. On the other hand, being direct in words is not as useful as being direct in actions. Even if you are trying to save time, don't be too direct when you talk to others. Stay soft and light. Find your own perfect combination of tact and honesty, and you will gain the respect of those you meet along the way.

In closing, I'll be short and sweet—do what you have to do and get it done. Approach the day's activities with the goal of simplicity. And then just do it. Other people will appreciate you as a person who gets things done.

Time to Appreciate

WHERE IS EVERYONE RUNNING? Most people really don't think about what they do. They just do it. Other people are too relaxed. They live life in slow motion. They only think about themselves in that particular moment. Why should life have to be like either of these? I'd like to see people somewhere in the middle.

Treat each day as an individual occurrence. Give each day a feeling of its own. Don't take for granted that another week is beginning and it will soon end, followed by another month, and another year. This way you won't move so quickly through life that you miss it. But also remember that you have only so much time. Don't waste a day because you are too tired to make use of it.

Most of the time, life is made up of your daily routine, but if you see these routines as purposeful, they won't be so difficult. Life is all about how much you appreciate it. Everyone must do things they don't want to, but some people see everything as a means to their end, a dream or goal. In this way, everything you do has value.

Take nothing for granted. Life is full of surprises. So take advantage of each day. At the end of each day, ask yourself: What have you accomplished? Are you satisfied? Could you have done more with your time? Looking back, you can realize what is important to you, and what you should move away from. You may even want to keep a diary of daily events, if not for memory, then just to recap the events of the day to feel you have made good use of your time.

Appreciate the people and things around you. Live and enjoy one day at a time. Take advantage of life, nature, and the good things around you. Don't wake up so many years later to find out that the years have gone by and you have missed out.

Traditions

Several years ago my community center presented a play called *Generations*. This play was seen by thousands of people in my community and was a huge success. As you may guess, the play was about the history of the community, beginning with my ancestors' immigration to the United States in the early 1900s. It included each generation which had lived in my community since then, right up to the present.

You can imagine why it was such a success. I, my friends and my family were able to see ourselves and our history reenacted for us. Looking back on that moment, I realize that what makes that history so special to me, is the beautiful tradition which is interwoven in every story and every street I walk across.

The definition of tradition is the delivery of opinions, doctrines, rites and customs from generation to generation. But this doesn't truly describe the richness of tradition behind the customs which I perform, and which my family has been performing for many centuries.

To know what your traditions stand for is to enjoy what you have. Just think about it. By appreciating and observing your tradition, you are sharing all the beautiful customs that your grandparents, and their grandparents have brought with them through their lives. They are sharing a piece of history with you, that you can also carry during the following years.

My religion is the basis of many of my customs. It is something that I can hold onto that is mine to appreciate and enjoy throughout my life. I feel very fortunate to live in a community with such a history of tradition. The roots of my family have been firmly established in America since the turn of the century.

But this is not always the case. Tradition can be expanded to mean so much more. The habits you have might have started out as customs which have been repeated so often they became everyday things. Perhaps you have a specific superstition you observe because it was told to you by our grandfather who was told by his grandfather. Even certain fundamental traits of characters such as honesty, compassion, courage, and perseverance can be virtues that you train your-self to have. It is what you are taught to respect when you are younger that becomes what you want to see in yourself and in those around you.

Tradition is like a ribbon which has woven itself into daily life and beyond. It can teach you about the way things used to be, but also about the way things are. It has so much to offer you, if you just take the time to listen. Never forget that not everything can be learned from a book. Some types of knowledge exist only in the deep hollows of the mind.

A few years later a play called *Celebrations* was presented by the same community center. This was really a continuation of the last one. It was about the customs and traditions which have existed in my community for almost a hundred years. It was about the holiday I observe, and the tradition that I cele-brate. A quote from *Celebrations* says it all: "Our lives get richer as treasures of the present add to memories of the past."

Power of Prayer

WHEN YOU SEE SOMEONE IN PAIN, it makes you flinch. When someone is crying, doesn't it make you a little sad? Being sensitive towards the next person is an excellent characteristic to have. Showing compassion for someone in their time of need is the most important sign of support.

Once there was an automobile accident in our community, in which four out of the five teenagers involved were hurt and rushed to the local hospital. One of the injured arrived at the hospital in critical condition. Within 12 hours a standing room crowd of 700 women gathered to pray in the local synagogue. That same evening almost 400 men continued to pray for the recovery of the innocent victims of the car accident.

Never before had so many people and families been touched by an incident like this. Compassion had found its way into the hearts of my community. Friends, family, and neighbors all joined together to recognize this amazing emotion. They addressed their compassion and shared it with those around them.

A young man who had organized the evening prayer went to visit the parents of the most critically injured. He told them of the concern that the people had. He described for this man that compassion had filtered into the hearts of men and women of the community, and they had joined together to express their deep concern and hope that everything would be all right.

The father looked up and asked, "What time had they been praying?" The young man, slightly surprised by the question replied, "from 6:30 to 7:30 P.M." With that the father broke down and cried. But then the young man noticed that though tears ran down his face, the father was smiling. The father looked at the young man and said, "The doctor came to visit us at 7 to say that they were very hopeful. They think he'll be OK."

The prayers of the people were being accepted. The compassion and feelings of such a large number of people had been answered in a very swift manner. Unity of feeling was spontaneous. Emotions were high. You can say that those people that took part in prayer are blessed in a way they might not even know.

There was no guarantee. There never is. You can never know for certain the extent to which prayer played a role. However, all the teenagers involved in the accident were released from the hospital within two weeks. Perhaps that fact speaks for itself.

My community understood the meaning of compassion as it was demonstrated. May your prayers always be answered and may you be blessed with happiness and health for generations to come.

Patience is a Virtue

Have you ever had a conversation with another person, and the other person continuously interrupts you, causing you to lose your train of thought? When this happens, don't you find yourself wondering if the person is even listening to what you have to say or just thinking about what they want to say next? A good example can be made when, in a classroom, a discussion is going on and a member of the class asks the same question that has already been answered. You know that this individual was not even listening to what was being said.

You can think of many instances where your own impatience has gotten the better of you. One case that comes to mind and affects a lot of people are traffic jams. Many roadways are almost like parking lots these days. It's one of the easiest opportunities to lose your patience. A good remedy in this particular case which has helped me, is to remind yourself that losing your temper will not change the situation. By keeping yourself calm, you can better assess the situation, appreciate the positives and the negatives, and make the most of it.

Patience is a tricky thing, and it's getting very hard to come by. Most people want the answer yesterday. But you can learn to have more patience. The first step is to learn how to calm your nerves before you lose it. Control of one's mind is essential. Just because someone loses it, is no excuse to follow suit. You will set the example by just being calm in a situation where patience will rule. Apply this philosophy to any situation and you will be a winner every time. Patience is an accomplishment that you can be proud of.

Having been in many meetings in my lifetime, I have found that the most ineffective people are those that jump the gun. They do not have the patience to hear someone else out. This can be very disruptive when trying to get a point across. But I didn't always understand this. I remember back in the years when I first came into the family business, how decisions were delayed. I could never understand it. I later realized that with the proper patience, time would pass and well thought out decisions could be made. That way no one felt rushed or pushed in any one direction. Somehow things would develop on there own as well.

When you are having a conversation with someone and you cut them off by interrupting to say something that was on your mind that had no relevance, you probably will not hear what the other person was going to say or how important it was. By interrupting the other person, you cause them to lose their train of thought. Think about it. How important was your impatient interruption? Patience allows you to listen and learn. Just think how hard a child works to get the attention and approval of their parents. The more patience and understanding you give a child, the happier you will be with the results. By taking the time to really listen to them, you will be giving your child what they really need, and they will learn not to be impatient themselves.

When I started writing this article, I could not finish it. I thought I lost my patience, but I really didn't. I learned a lot more about patience in the process. You really have to let experience teach you. But it will give you a better understanding of people, and also teach you to be more tolerant and patient of others. By just being conscious of being patient, you too will be much happier with yourself as well as others around you. It's almost like saying you have improved your whole outlook on life by doing nothing but being patient! In conclusion, be a virtuoso with the virtue of patience.

Leave Nothing To Chance

THEY HAPPENED TO BE at the right place at the right time. Where have you heard that before? If it sounds too good to be true, then it probably is. Because, in reality, you are the reason for being at the right place at the right time. Buying a lottery ticket and hoping to win the big prize at great odds is leaving things to chance. But in your day to day life, people that are successful are people that make things happen.

People are blessed with the ability to be creative. Human beings are born with the tools and the ability with which to accomplish many things during the course of a lifetime. But it is up to you to take the ball, and run with it until you reach your goals. You have to discover your own unique gifts, and find out how to use them to your own advantage.

Leaving nothing to chance is almost like waiting in line for your turn to come. It can be waiting for that customer to walk in the door, or that girl or guy to come into your life. But if you always remain the catalyst of all your actions, your time will come. You will achieve your goals, so long as you keep working towards them.

I find that making things happen is one of the most important aspects of my career. I make the phone call to a prospective buyer. He or she will return my call, but it is up to me to start a conversation. One thing leads to another, and then I can make an appointment to meet, and consummate a transaction. Who knows? Maybe I will be making the greatest sale of my life.

You can use the same attitude for love. It is up to you to get out there. It is up to you to make the decision of staying home and watching T.V. or going to that party. Perhaps some people are meant to be together. But if you wait for chance to bring you together, you might not ever meet that special him or her. Fate has a lot to do, sometimes you must give it a hand!

In everyday life, you must work to make things happen. You really have to pay your dues and put in the time to see results. How much can you say for "being at the right place at the right time"? In reality, you make things happen every day. You help to create your own destiny. Destiny does not create you.

The mind is powerful when put to good use. Some people use the art of creativity more than others. Some people must work a little harder for what they want. But remember that some of the most successful people have failed before becoming successful. So even if you take a chance, and it seems that you have lost, hang in there because happiness might be just around the corner.

By calling on as many people as you can in a day, you will increase the possibility that success will find you. Put some bait, on a hook, and a fish might come sailing along and take a bite. Without any bait on the hook, the fish will have no reason to bite.

Creating your own chances, will enhance the possibility of your being in the right place at the right time. Don't sell yourself short by waiting for things to happen. Go out, and make it happen, before someone else does.

Leave nothing to chance!

Memories and Tradition

AT THE LAST MINUTE, I was asked to take my five year old grandson Charles to the last All Star game of the millennium in Boston. We had to rush to catch the 5:30 shuttle in order to get to the park by 8 o'clock to see the home run hitting contest held the night before the game. Well, we made it.

We saw history being made that day. There was Fenway Park, and the Green Monster, the wall out in left field. This was where Babe Ruth started out and where the last 400 hitter, Ted Williams, played his whole career.

The stadium was filled to capacity. As the name of each home run slugger was announced, you could see a wave of fans cheering and applauding throughout the park. It was really something to see. Mark McGwire of the St. Louis Cardinals, who set the record for most home runs in a season last year, stole the show. He hit a record thirteen home runs. One caught the lights way up above the Green Monster in left field. He hit the ball for over a mile with all his home runs combined.

He was, of course, my grandson's favorite. After the home run hitting contest we went to an outdoor party given by Major League Baseball. My grandson went right to the front of the line at the batting cage. Before I knew it, he was swinging at the pitches with his helmet on. It was a real blast as a grandfather to see my grandson in all his glory. He just loves to play ball like his daddy and his grandpa.

Day two gave us the opportunity to witness a magnificent pre-game ceremony. The presentation of the greatest living players in baseball came together in the final All Star game of the 1900's. The likes of Stan Musiel, Willie Mays, Bob Feller and Hank Aaron were amongst the many honored as part of an all-century team in a very moving pre-game tribute. The fans went wild when Boston's own Ted Williams was honored as the greatest living hitter of the century. He waved to the fans in a golf cart that drove him around the park and to the pitchers mound. It was a very touching moment as all the Old Timers and the All Stars gathered around Ted Williams to congratulate him.

As Donna Summers finished singing the National Anthem, four AWAC jets zoomed over the ball park, causing it to shake. The Boston ace, Pedro Martinez, set a record by striking out the first three batters at the start of the game. Each time he did so, a roar went up from the crowd, rising above the stadium. The fans were really stupendous, they showed such support and enthusiasm.

The whole time I was sitting in Fenway Park, I kept thinking about what an enormous history exists in baseball. The fans, the players, and that shining baseball diamond are all wrapped together in a beautiful tradition which has existed for decades. As I watched the game, what I was really seeing was all the memories which were like so many grains of sand on the pitcher's mound. I saw Babe Ruth running the bases, or Mickey Mantle taking a swing. Then I turned to look at my grandson. I saw myself, with that same wide-eyed expression. I remembered that feeling of hero-worship that comes of being a little boy watching great men do what you could only dream of doing.

With the new millennium right around the corner, and all the fears of what will happen, it's nice to know that this great American tradition will live on. And as I ordered my grandson another box of Cracker Jacks®, I knew that he would do the same thing one day. Only he would be sitting in my place, watching the young boy sitting next to him.

Index

About the Author

CHARLES S. HADDAD is the chairman of Haddad Apparel, Inc., America's number one children's clothier.

Born in New York City and currently living at the New Jersey shore, he has worked in the family business for forty-six years. When the company was started in the thirties by his grandfather, his father and his uncles, it imported lace goods from China. After World War II, the company moved in to Japan, Taiwan, and Hong Kong. Like many thriving family companies, Haddad has changed with each successive generation. The company went into children's licensed apparel beginning in 1980, and today it has such brands as Bugle Boy, Harley-Davidson, Avirex, Weebok and Reebok, as well as sports and character licenses.

As the chairman of a company that does business throughout the world, Charles S. Haddad has circled the globe for business and for pleasure. He has written *Thoughts From The Heart* to share the insights that decades of business experience and family life have taught him.